AN EVER-PRESENT THREAT

CONTENTS

INTRODUCTION

Welcome ladies & gentlemen, to the world as you've never quite seen it before, through the freakish lens of 'The Snow Hare!' It's a rather theatrical pen name, but it comes with a backstory. A couple of years ago my extended family decided to get into a bit of genealogy, looking up the old family tree. & it turns out I'm directly descended from the notorious grave robber William Hare, of the infamous Burke & Hare murders! Perhaps that goes some way to explaining why I ended up voluntarily hospitalised, to stop myself from becoming a spree killer. Something in the blood? That was almost twenty years ago now, & since then I've undergone a series of radical transformations! I've worked for over a decade in the Care Industry, on suicide hotlines. Counselling alcoholics, bereavement, & drug addicts, specialising in Personal Development. I'm a SSSC registered, university post-graduate, working with violently disturbed individuals, on the borderline of permanent institutional care. I've overcome drug addiction, alcoholism, quit smoking, lost over three stone, & I'm on a mission to help reduce the unnecessary suffering in the world! Specifically trying to reach out to those who walk the razor's edge, as I once did, those who are nihilistic, suicidal, & angry at existence itself.

Recently I released the first in the 'Optimal Path' series, a trilogy of self-help books designed to permanently alter people's perceptions. Created as a lifeline for those who find themselves in extreme isolation, contemplating suicide, or violence toward others. Simplifying & condensing countless hours of training & research, this series is meant to enrich your life, instil a sense of purpose, & self-belief. These books could not be more heartfelt! Writing them was emotionally exhausting, quite literally to the point of physical collapse. Since then I've been working on 'The Poetry of Chaos' series, which is filled with dark fantasies of home invasions, dungeons, shark attacks, & serial killers. I've broken through countless barriers, emotionally, artistically, & I now feel free to express myself on a completely new level.

In truth I don't really know what this book is going to be about, that's just something we'll have to find out along the way. & that's the challenge, which makes this a scary proposition, because I intend to keep pushing myself further & further. Though it's only fair to warn you that it will doubtless be profane, irreverent, & ultra-violent. But I can guarantee you that it won't be like anything you've ever encountered before!

(Disclaimer)

Now that the book is finished & I'm looking back over it, I can see the overall picture which it creates. Each chapter has a different vibe, mostly playful, with different styles of writing. I want to make these books accessible to quite a wide audience, but I do go into depth on things such as psychological defence mechanisms, so if you are struggling with the density of technical information, then I won't blame you if you choose to skip ahead. The 2nd half of chapter 7 especially, is packed with advice, & perhaps from a self-help perspective it's one of the most important parts of the book. But chapter 8 is a short story, completely different to everything that's gone before. What I'm saying is, I want you to enjoy this book without feeling overwhelmed! So, think of it like listening to a CD, don't give up, skip forward, till you find a track you like!

Or use it as a meditation, & train yourself to focus! Not that I'm challenging your reading skills you understand? Or calling you Chicken? Heavens forbid!

JUST PEACHY

Trapped under a perpetual slate grey sky, this city of mine. It's not, not really, global warming has done for that. Blistering summers with endless blue in all directions, but they are still slate grey to me. & this is not depression I'm describing, but an affection. Because all I ever remember was drizzle, slapping you in the face, day after day, throughout my childhood. I refuse to acknowledge the sun, the blue skies, because the drizzle's what makes this place home. It's part of the essential nature of this city, along with the chip shop related heart attacks & the knife crime, it's something to feel perversely proud of. 'Murder capital of Western Europe?' You're damn fucking right it is!

& out of nowhere the blade is under my neck, whispered threats in my ear as I'm drawn backward, off balance, as I'm laid down upon a tomb. This is no flight of fancy, in the darkness of the Necropolis, is where I so very nearly met my fate. & he's counting down from 10, 9, 8, his associates, a group of three are standing over his shoulder, more scared than I am, in my drunken stupor. & I'm looking him square in the eye, he's told me what he's going to do, this total stranger. I am literally going to die, & he's not merely counting down to put the fear in me, before he lets me go. I can see in his face that he's building himself up, he's readying himself to slit my throat.

I'd be lying if I didn't admit there wasn't a hint of peach to the grey skies today, but that's not what you want to hear is it, 'the grim north' with a hint of peach. & I was out at the cinema in one of these malls recently, I'd been there several times before. When I suddenly realise, hold on, this is the old Pollok centre! Where I used to come swimming as a kid. Always with my head in the clouds, I'd step into the car & hey presto, you're in Inverness, or the Lake District, or wherever. I had no idea how to get anywhere, that was grown up stuff. Then as the years roll past, it's the bus into town, & then the train to wherever & out of public transport my understanding of the world expands. Then after nights of drunken excess I'd find myself stumbling through the city streets making these connections, 'oh right, so that's how these two different bits join together.' & to me this shiny big cookie cutter mall just appeared out of fucking nowhere. Like I give a fuck? But hold on a second, if this really is the Pollok centre, then where are all the grim-faced punters? The ones which I remember populating this place since childhood? & in that very moment the scales fell away from my eyes, they were all around me, the gurning faces of the unwashed masses, but tarted up, gentrified, in exactly the same way as the fucking mall itself. It was a reality that I couldn't unsee. These were traditional working-class people, a large percentage of whom were probably unemployed, but they were all smartly turned out, in their Debenhams garb, in a way in which they never gave a fuck about before. & it all just seemed so fucking fake!

They've taken away all the old café's, I wouldn't even be able to tell you where you could get a decent all-day breakfast around here. & obviously nobody gives a fuck or they wouldn't have closed down, but it's the sign of a culture in atrophy. It's dying off, one greasy spoon at a time. & I'm not entirely averse to Americanisation, in that I'm quite content with a cheeseburger, & an Avengers movie. But there's a certain loss of identity, which comes with mass commodification, which extends beyond the overpriced boutiques. It's not a superficial thing, it extends into the collective psyche, & it comes at a cost! Yes, everything's shinier, but it's also more sterile, colder. The corporations are sucking the marrow out of our bones, & with it goes our sense of community. & why is that important? It's the ability to communicate on a deep personal level, something which the kids brought into this world will never know they lost.

7, 6, 5, our eyes are connected. & he can see something in me that perhaps scares him slightly. There's part of me that wants him to do it! Come on you cunt, fucking kill me, right here, in the city of the dead. Because I've so very nearly killed myself before, through hanging, slit wrists, police taking me down off rooftops. You're doing me a favour, don't pussy out, be a man & fucking do it! But there's was no flinching in him. There was some deep pain, some unhinged lunacy in his soul, just as there was in mine. In that moment it was a complete inevitability, it was happening! Without question, between the pair of us, it was happening!

& maybe I'm over romanticising something which is inherently flawed, but when you love something, it is in part because of the flaws. & I love this city, make no mistake about it, I love it deeply! Glasgow, with the Gothic Revival style of its Victorian architecture, is exquisite. Buildings constructed in the late 19th century, with an emphasis on the ornate. Grand, tall designs, with an abundance of pointed arches, gargoyles, & the occasional flying buttress. I love the grim, grey, gritty, fuck you of it all. Because it's my home, & I've got the scars to prove it!

4, 3, & the group of guys at his back are frozen in place, they are doing fuck all about it. I'm about to get my throat cut, & bleed out in this graveyard, & they are all going to be accessories to murder, because they haven't the balls to step up & do something to stop it. & out of the darkness, in that opportune moment, somebody screams,

'HEY, WHAT ARE YOU DOING?!!'

I'd just met the guy that night, a ned amongst goths, out drinking in a graveyard. The kind of guy that the world overlooks, but I could see that he had a good soul. So, I made the deliberate attempt to make some sort of connection. & as we'd all traipsed out of the place, I'd lagged behind, & he doubled back to find me surrounded by guys, not really knowing what was going on, & shouted. So, with my attacker entirely focused on me, his knife pressed to my throat, that tiny little break in his concentration was all it took, for me to pull the blade away from my throat.

I had a student many years ago, who I was teaching martial arts, primarily kickboxing, with a few more exotic techniques thrown in. & one day a drug dealer pulled a knife on him, & he used the Kotegaeshi wrist lock that I had taught him. Took the blade off him, pushed him into the corner of a doorway & headbutted him. Then had the luxury of threatening him, before letting him go, & watching him scamper away up the street. I had control of the wrist & was assessing my options. If it was a one on one, I would have taken the blade off him, in exactly the same fashion. But the problem was the guys behind him, so I did something crazy, I let go of his wrist.

The squirrels are out & scampering today. Without leaves on the trees they are easy to spot, & I watch as people stroll down the street. They don't see me, because I'm looking down from a window above. & I don't know if you've ever noticed this but the average human's plain of awareness is only really two dimensional, they see only what's on the flat. Perhaps if we evolved in the age of the pterodactyl, we'd make more effort to look up, but as it is...

But spotting squirrels? There's no excuse, they are closer than I am. Inattentional blindness, that's what I call it, not giving a fuck you could say. But the problem with that is that it becomes an ingrained habit & soon, not giving a fuck will become an automated response. It takes effort to open your awareness, to be emotionally sensitive, to care. & I can more than understand why you would want to numb yourself, as I've said elsewhere, I've spent most of my adult life trying to numb away the pain of existence, mostly with alcohol. & I said in the introduction that I don't know what this book is going to be about, & that's not entirely true, because there's a certain question that's rolling around in my subconscious that I want to explore. & it's about overcoming fear, instead of choosing to be numb, allowing yourself to be vulnerable, being able to communicate, & then being able to connect with other people. Because I've been on a journey of self-discovery, over decades, I've radically changed my outlook, I've come to learn so much through interaction with others, through reading, education, work, sociology, psychology, self-help, meditation, psychedelic visions, I've steeped myself in these things for years. I've had some deep revelations, & I've found peace on a level that I never imagined possible. I've also charted the entire process, so that those who are lost in the same way that I was, can use my experience to help transform their lives. But how can you truly, deeply, connect with people? & what are the barriers which stop you from doing that? That is in part the challenge which I hope to address in this book, & with this book. Because I want to find some way to get people to read it. So that they at least know that a book like 'The Optimal Path' exists, that they know that it's possible to drag yourself out of suicidal depression, & there's somebody out there who genuinely cares! Before they choose to commit suicide, or perform some kind of unthinkable atrocity.

I have control of the wrist of the hand which is holding the blade, & I let it go. Because if I go for the Kotegaeshi I risk exposing my back & who knows what kind of weapons these guys are carrying? As it stands, I have one thing to my advantage & that is that the guy with the knife creates a barrier between me & them. He swings the knife at my face, in a high overhand arc, & I lean back as far as I physically can, & the tip of the blade catches me at the corner of my left eye socket, passes within millimetres of my eye, & slices a thin cut along the side of my nose, without causing any serious damage. Lying back on the flat tomb I bring one foot up to his chest, less to push him away, & more to give me the momentum to roll backward off the tomb, & run in the opposite direction. & as I sprint through the darkness, as fast as I possibly can, we come to the scary part.

& though you may well fear the creation of artificial intelligence, the age of the machines has already begun. Everybody is plugged in, slaves to the beep, the text, the update, the notification. It's inescapable, wired to your deepest impulses. Sex, violence, fast food at the touch of a button. It's convenient, it's ubiquitous, & if you're not involved, if you're not on social media, then you're some kind of freak! There's something wrong with you! You are hiding! Because everyone has a smartphone, which is linked in to every possible kind of distraction you can think of, it's all right there, at the touch of a button. But what's the reciprocal nature of this relationship. Where does the machine start & end? Because kids now get born twice, the second birth is an online avatar, a psychological illness made mandatory by the culture into which they are born. & it isn't real, just one big computer game, but they are killing themselves, behind locked doors. They are stretched thin in a charade to present themselves as some aspirational 2d character that photoshops out their flaws. & don't you dare fuck up! Or say something inappropriate, because then it's out there forever! & there's no blocking out the bullies, the haters, the trolls, night or day. It's a system that relies on negative feedback, clickbait journalism, the snake eating its tail. This is the death of truth, the end of articulation, community, connection, sold out, soulless, isolation, & suffering!

I can't see out of my left eye, I think I'm blind, it's just filled with blood but I don't have time to wipe it, because I'm running downhill as fast as I fucking can, with them closing in behind me, & that's not the scary part. I come to a junction, I need to turn left, but the ground is covered in grit, & I plant both my feet & slide. I spent my entire childhood hitting punching bags, throwing javelins, or throwing balls around, & there's barely a limb or a joint that I haven't fucked up at one point or another. & my right knee is no exception. & as I'm sliding, I can feel it starting to give way. It was one of those time slowing down moments, fuck, fuck, fuck, fuck! Knee gives in, I'm going down & I'm dead, that simple. & I can feel the cartilage squeaking, the ligaments on the verge of snapping. I'm trying to ease off it, but all my weight is bearing down, as I try to maintain my balance, in this seemingly endless slide. In that moment I'm no longer even thinking about the eye. & the knee somehow holds, by the same kind of millimetres as the blade that missed my eye, it holds! & I'm off again & running. Later on, when I'm looking in the hospital mirror, I have a big grin on my face. Because I came that close! By seconds & millimetres, I was that close, not just to losing the eye, but to death!

I later heard that somebody chucked the guy off a flyover bridge. I can only imagine that he brought it upon himself. I don't bear any grudges over that incident, because I don't take it personally. To me it was just a case of being in the wrong place at the wrong time. There are any number of homicidal nutcases out there. That guy was like a force of nature, like getting caught up in a hurricane, shit happens! Especially around here. Not only have I had a knife to my throat, I had one over my heart. I've been bottled, & subsequently disarmed people with bottles, twice. One of those guys later got done for armed robbery. I've been hit over the head with an iron bar, I dropped someone with a spinning kick to the head, punched someone in the nuts, choked someone out with a standing guillotine, had to relocate my shoulder, so that I could punch someone in the face. I once broke someone's leg with a flying body scissors, & at one point I had a team of guys intent on coming after me with samurai swords. These are just some of the incidents I can remember off the top of my head, & I have never in my life once started a fight.

& anybody can sit behind a keyboard & make up fictional stories about all the belts they've won, & fights they've had. So, instead I'm going to tell you how much I love martial arts in a way that these meatheads would never think of. When Amanda Nunes knocked out Cris Cyborg I cried, because it was one of the most beautiful things I'd ever seen. Months later, re-watching the fight, I cried again. I bear no ill will to Cyborg, I think she's a legend, but seeing someone come out & face the dragon like that, Amanda Nunes is a real hero! I have friends that watch the UFC who don't even rate women's MMA, genuinely tears rolling down my cheeks! It's the best way I can think to express my relationship with martial arts, but my background is Shotokai, kickboxing, judo, silat, & bits of aikido, traditional ju-jitsu, & more recently what would be considered MMA. I used to be all about the flashy Taekwondo style spinning kicks, now I prefer the technical elements of dirty boxing & Brazilian ju-jitsu. But I spend more time these days with swordplay & meditation, lots of meditation.

& though I'm sitting here criticising contemporary culture, technology & all of that, I'm not blind to the fact that the very existence of this book is in large part due to the marvels of modern technology. I'm not even going to pretend I'm not a hypocrite, that I'm not flawed in exactly the same ways as everybody else, but I'll put my flaws up front & wear my scars proudly because I believe in being real. I believe in facing up to fear, finding the dragon, & facing it down! Because that's how you discover your potential, that's how you become the person you were destined to be! & we all have our demons, we all have issues which we'd rather not address, but it's that kind of avoidance which makes us self-medicate, running away, making ourselves numb, using gadgets as a way to distract us from the real world. & I want to know how you can reach through to someone, to make them really fucking hear you!!? Beyond the inattentional blindness, beyond the button pushing automaton that they've turned themselves into. Because everything becomes categorised, instantly, unconsciously, you can't present a thing to a person without them already having a preconceived notion about what it is they are looking at. & this way they can ignore just about anything. So, I want to present you with something you don't recognise, something new, which makes you stop, makes you think. & the way to do it is through being real, being open, being honest, giving you my unfiltered truth.

& I'm not writing to the beat, & you can fuck your iambic pentameter, rhyming couplets et al. I don't give a fuck about any form of writing which has ever gone before, this isn't an imitation. All I'm doing is writing from the heart, letting it flow, showing you the colour of my soul. Pages drenched in tears, silent screams, & the deepest apprehension. Because I write in a way that scares the living fuck out of me! I push myself into disturbing places, to the point of suicidal ideation, till I've collapsed to the ground, vomiting on myself! & the intention is to go deeper, perpetually deeper, uncovering what is hidden, making myself vulnerable. Because I've spent years running from my pain, limiting myself, holding myself back. & I don't want you to go through that, running in circles, filled with self-loathing, feeling shame for something you should not.

I want you to be able to hear me, in a way that you never expected could ever happen, but in a way you've always secretly yearned. Someone who's not presenting a front, obsessed with superficial bullshit, who isn't afraid to talk from the heart, & is grounded in something you deeply recognise. It's about being genuinely alive, fully present. When I write I'm perpetually seeking a certain state, a subtle frequency, filled with passion, where the tears flow freely down my cheeks. It's the purest elation, an overflow of emotion, total clarity. When it feels like there's something of incredible significance happening. That I'm somehow piercing through the slate grey skies to make a true connection with someone who has convinced themselves that they are destined to spend an eternity in isolation. Convinced that they will never be truly listened to, or understood, by another human being, no matter how hard they try. I want to show you that it is possible, to be heard, & seen, that you are not alone, & that you never were!

Because I recognise what a state of desperation is like, I know all too well what it's like to suffer the insomnia of homicidal rage, to be overwhelmed with hatred for everybody, & everything. I know what it's like to simply want to die, for it all to end. I know what it's like to give up on everything, because it feels like everything has already given up on you. To be surrounded by people who you can't trust, who just make you feel more alone, to be ostracised by those you once loved. To have your best friend turn their back on you. To be left alone, convinced that you were a freak, destined to spend eternity as an outcast, never accepted, forever on the outside looking in. I know what it's like to feel like you have to pretend like you are something you are not, just so that people won't see you. I know what it's like to have loved, & to have it ripped away from you. I know what it's like when everything collapses, problem on top of problem, threats on all sides, complications on top of heart ache, when you can't envisage any possible way that life can continue beyond this point. Anger, betrayal, loss, self-hatred, humiliation, total despair, to be completely & totally broken. To the point that all you want to do is kill as many people as you physically can, & that becomes an all-consuming fixation, that you carry night & day. Crossing over into an insanity where you feel like the world isn't even real, & your actions have no consequence. In a living nightmare. I know what that's like, when hospital is the only option left, to save the world from what you might do. I know what all of that is like.

So, now that my life is stable, & I'm at peace. My mind is calm & clear. I'm in a healthy routine, sleeping properly, looking after myself, not drinking. Working. Being creative. & I've faced up to the demons that caused all of those problems in the first place. & now even regularly cry tears of elation, should I sit in smug self-satisfaction? No, it's time to roll up my sleeves & get to work, because the world is filled with people going through exactly the same kind of problems which I faced & overcame. & so much of it is avoidable, so much of the suffering that goes on in our unspoken inner worlds is entirely avoidable. But we sit in silence, unable to communicate because we are afraid to appear weak, afraid to acknowledge our emotions. Unable to truly connect with one another, in any meaningful way, beyond small talk & common interests. & I know I'm repeating myself from other books but what I want to create for you here is a space where you feel accepted, despite the flaws you aren't even willing to acknowledge. A place where it's ok to be the real you, the weird, & broken you. I want you to share in this place with me, like it was from a half-forgotten childhood dream. Back when life was simple, a most treasured memory. A sincere untainted feeling of security & contentment. Regardless of how fucked up the rest of your life might be, a little bubble of calm, where there is no stress, pressure, or judgement, a place where we can truly be free.

There was a time, when I felt I'd lost all connection to the world, & any relationships I did have I was self-sabotaging. It became a truth that I was choosing to create. I was forcing it into reality, & I became incredibly bitter. I second guessed everybody's actions. & filled with mistrust, people became awkward around me, creating a vicious circle, where my paranoia intensified. It was only recently that I came to realise that I had developed a fear of over-attachment, having had felt betrayed by friends in the past, I got locked into a habit of unintentionally burning bridges. Deliberately ostracising myself, often simply by being too blunt, or honest. Failing to keep secrets, passing on gossip that I knew would set the vineyard ablaze. Being completely direct with someone who was putting up a façade, attacking people at an existential level, I had serious issues! Honesty can be the most vicious weapon when handled with malice.

But a biased perspective can create any form of reality it wants, the truth with which you torture yourself may in fact be bullshit, a total misconception. But if you refuse to face up to whatever it is, that misconception will persist indefinitely. & the reason I want to create this space is so that you have a place to explore the unaddressed misconceptions which have been quietly torturing you for years. The things which cause self-sabotaging behaviours, self-medication, anger issues, etc. After many years of personal development, I don't feel isolated, I feel connected, to everybody & everything, & my writing is an expression of that, I'm just trying to get the rest of you up to speed. I want to help people look past the superficial narrative that's been presented to them by society, to see the deeper bond that already exists between us all. You see, I'm not trying to make a connection, just trying to draw your attention to a connection that was already there!

BEING VULNERABLE

If, in the unlikely event I should one day become rich & famous, I reserve the right to have whatever kind of freaky sex I like, without scandal or judgement. Let's just get that out of the way right now! As long as it's between two consenting adults, or three, or four, or however many you can convince to engage in your shenanigans, it's not really anybody else's business, unless they are a camera tech, or a sound engineer. Look, we're missing the point here, you can all just fuck off! With your opinionated judgemental bullshit! That's what I'm saying to you, it's better to start off on the wrong foot, that's all I'm saying. I want to start off bellow derision, & preferably stay there, thank you very much. What's the point of being rich & famous anyway, if not for the freaky sex? It should in fact be a scandal if you're rich & famous, & you're not having freaky sex. Because then you're just letting the side down! Look at this self-righteous douche, all that money & fame, & he thinks he's too good for it? What I'm trying to say is, no doubt I'll step on your toes, & if these books were ever to enter into the public consciousness there'd no doubt be people just waiting to label me, my opinions, my standpoint. So, let's just cut the bullshit, shall we? There's only one label you need, & it's **'FREAK!'**

We don't need to start getting grandiose, putting on heirs & graces. I've accepted this reality a long time ago, I just ain't normal, never have been, & I've unquestionably suffered as a result. & it's taken me a long time to see the positives, to find the utility in the things which make me different, but they are the things today of which I am most proud. I've always been somewhat uncategorizable in any number of ways. I live in the city; my dad was raised on a farm on the other side of the country. I have an accent that isn't quite like anybody around me, slightly American for some unknown reason. It means that people have to pay close attention if they want to figure out what I'm saying, but they rarely do. I've always had a foot in two worlds, working class, middle class, & kind of been rejected by both. My feminine side is pronounced, so much so that masculinity always felt like a pretence, like I was a butch dyke in a man's body. & that's not an issue unless I'm open about it, which tends to make guys particularly uncomfortable. I've always asked a different kind of question, been looking for deeper conversations. Fads & trends always passed me by. I'm somewhere on the autistic spectrum, I have a split personality when I drink, & at my worst I've had what Dr's have described as prolonged psychotic episodes. I've always been oversensitive, but that's something which I've been able to harness & embrace. I'm like the canary in the coal mine, I'm here to warn you of imminent dangers. It's like I've fucked with every possible aspect of my life till I've found out exactly how it looks from every angle, so that I can break down what it means to be a human being in every aspect, from personal experience. I have for example been ostracised for being gay, although I'm not. It's a horrible thing to do to someone, to try & make them feel ashamed of who they are. But when people don't know how to label you, they come up with their own simplifications. & the truth is I couldn't give a fuck if you did think I was gay, & maybe just opening the chapter like this will mean I lose potential readers, but I'd rather lose a few homophobes, if it means I can connect more deeply with those who have felt ostracised their entire lives.

Prejudice is something which is ingrained deep within our culture, & I'm strongly averse to racism, misogyny, homophobia, & any kind of hatred of that nature, regardless of however my words are wilfully misinterpreted in the future. Yet I don't expect everybody out there to share my views. & I want to connect with as wide an audience as possible, even those who feel deep hatred for other social groups. Because there have been any number of active shooters out there who have specifically targeted gay clubs, & members of different religious faiths. I want to talk to as many human beings on this planet as physically possible. I want these books to permeate popular culture on a global level, & it's not for the purposes of freaky sex! It's to stop motherfuckers killing each other! It's to speak to the lonely, the isolated, the hurt, & angry souls, who feel like they have no other option but to lash out at the world. As I said in the last chapter, it's to draw your attention to the connection which we all share. To stop people from hurting each other, & themselves. Especially when it's pointless, & especially when it's avoidable.

& I genuinely don't want to make myself the point of focus. I'm trying to do the opposite of that, hiding behind a pen name, writing in the shadows. & the purpose of this particular book is to introduce you to a growing library of material that's already available online, intended not just to educate but to entertain, so here's a little excerpt from 'The Poetry of Chaos,' which I particularly like.

'& a chocolate biscuit wrapper, riding an upward thermal has a momentary glimpse of godhood, looking down over the city streets at night. All the people no more than specks. & in between the buildings it falls, wafted gently along on the breeze. Flipping from the turbulence of a passing gull. This little lane is not what it once was. Ear drum popping dance clubs, pools of blood & broken glass among the cobbles. Everything gentrified, replaced with transgender toilets, which create exorbitant cues, hipsters exchanging homemade candles. Gone is the pissing trough, along with the gashed faces, & fumbled strobe lit fingerings. Now the bald bartender is rocking a plaited dwarven beard, a high fantasy creature, mixing drinks with a spinning underhand grip. It's service with panache!

The little sweetie wrapper floating between the legs, through the horde of people out on the street, looking up the skirts, & not a blade among them. But daggers in the eyes of the hot little tramps, walking about in their knickers, translucent dresses allow for the pretence of conformity. I didn't really leave the house in my underwear! Why does everyone keep staring at me? Self-hatred gives off mixed messages. & can you find a fucking seat in this place? & can you get to the bar, or hear the bartender over the throng? & how much did that cost, seriously? & soon all that will be left of this moment, this event, will be a ton of used bottles, discarded next to the meat curtains down a back alley. & bruised recollections of embarrassing encounters. But for now, it's an amber haze of fluid, ice cold, imported, draught. It's a glug of shiraz, & outside for a quick puff, the street filled with Turkish brothel flavoured vape smoke. & a pair of guys in two for one matching purple t-shirts trying to ingratiate themselves to the people outside, like a pair of narcs, they couldn't be more out of place. Meanwhile inside, a table filled with queens, queers, & dapper gents high fiving. This place is truly cosmopolitan! & there are a thousand games at play, people trying to influence, coerce, tease, or impress. You can barely hear yourself think, but it's better that way! Nobody came here to think, they came to imbibe, & forget, & it's working!

& though the Philip Larkin's of this world may stand outside the window, with their longing faces pressed to the glass, before casting their embittered eye over proceedings & calling fraud. Inside it's warm, it's joyous, & it's fun! A transient experience, a pointless endeavour, but it's fun & that's what counts. & the same thing underpins all of it. It's the reason for the alcohol, breaking down the barriers. It's the revealing clothes, it's in the banter, the laughter. It's connection. It's what they all want & need, it's why they are all here. & the young ones play their games, all super serious. & the old ones find confidence in the awareness, that it's all fucking irrelevant. If they have even the slightest bit of self-awareness, they know this isn't their world! Not anymore! But there's no time for anyone now, the pub's closing, it's club or taxi, them's yer choices! The little lane is slowly emptying, as people go on about their business, of further inebriation, drugs, fucking, kebab, or bed! & trapped flailing between the meat curtains, down a back alley is our little sweetie wrapper. & out comes the DJ & his pals, propped up with those extra little shots of tequila, after the lock-in. Spilling out into the night, & heading home! Trapped between the meat curtains, aren't we all?'

There's no hint of peach, to the slate grey skies today. This is nothing like the drizzle of my youth, as once again we're getting whipped off the tail end of a hurricane. I was lying awake in bed last night as the winds buffeted against the window, somewhere in the distance a wheelie bin crashes to the ground. It's so violent outside even the drunken punters stoating home have chosen to shut the fuck up, & it was a Friday night as well. You can picture their little windblown faces, leaning into a headwind, three steps forward, one to the side. & as I'm lying there unable to sleep, I'm amazed by quite how silent my mind has become. It wasn't always like this, & yet still, every now & again, especially when I'm tired, my mind will still pull me into the aforementioned 'bruised recollections of embarrassing encounters.' & these can often be from twenty years ago, or more. You know that squirmy feeling you get when your face blushes. & I grumble to myself, rolling over onto my opposite side, as though this physical act has some sort of symbolic significance, turning my back on the ghosts of a distant past. What does the world feel like on this side? & I'm greeted by a fresh cold pillow, & by the time I've snuggled myself back into a foetal position, the fleeting discomfort of the embarrassing memory has all but subsided. & they are almost entirely alcohol related. But it's something which fascinates me, the causal link between the emotional & the physiological. Tears of elation?

When you blush, there is a direct cause & effect. We have

a tendency to train ourselves into compulsive behaviours. Feel stressed? Self-medicate. It happens on impulse. There are times when I've been walking out a shop with bags filled with alcohol, wondering how the fuck it happened? Like a zombie with a debit card. More subtle is the long-term effects of stress, the kind of stuff that leads to cancer, & brain aneurisms. As well as active shooters, that's another thing I want to help society with by writing these books, just stress in general, & all the negative impacts it could potentially have on your life. So, to stop me from simply paraphrasing here's a little excerpt from 'The Optimal Path' as well.

'Life is an ongoing matter of diplomacy, between you & your work mates, with your loved ones, with your addictions, with yourself, between order & chaos. & there's no point living with buried resentments, it's like swallowing poison & waiting for the other person to get ill. All you are doing is inviting stress into your life, ulcers, strokes, heart attacks, this is not the life you want to lead.

Yet people fail to strategize their lives, to take time out to consider their goals, people don't try because they are afraid to fail, which is a sure way to inevitably fail. People don't like to limit their options, but that's exactly how you stop yourself from functioning optimally. You need some basic guidelines, because otherwise you're left with a vague, incalculable, potentially unlimited number of avenues, & most likely no idea what your goals should even be, let alone how to achieve them. It's paralysing. It takes courage to set off into the unknown, knowing you're destined for failure & rejection, but that's life, you've just got to stick with it till you get a basic grasp of what's going on. Then as time progresses you can start to diversify those strategies, add new tricks to your arsenal, & eventually you'll become a force to contend with, provided you can weather the setbacks with the appropriate attitude. & that's the difference at the end of the day, most of the time, it's the attitude which you take. Are you going to curl up into a ball & feel sorry for yourself? Or are you going to start to rebuild, & keep going after it? Because that's what you have to do to reach the tipping point.

They say recovery from addiction is like this, that all you've got to do is keep on trying. Fallen off the wagon? Set a date, & go again! Till eventually it seems to happen all by itself. The neurochemical receptors in your brain finally make that connection, that no! 'I don't want to do this anymore' & it becomes easy. That's kind of how I found it with alcohol. & I don't want to say these things to be sanctimonious, but I want people to know that one day, if you keep on trying, it'll become easy. But in the meantime, I have two words for you, 'envision alternatives.' This was a key phrase in my thinking around addiction, the idea that there are other options, a different path to the one which you are currently on.'

It'll probably not surprise you to hear that I took a lot of drugs back in the 90's. That is in part why I'm such an embarrassment to myself when I'm drunk, because I've lowered my boundaries, I'm too open. It works when I'm sat at a keyboard, but not so great when I'm drunk & surrounded by random strangers who want nothing to do with me. & from the outside there's a blanket approach of saying drugs are bad, & that there is a clear line between those who take drugs, & those who don't. & don't get me wrong there are obviously full-blown junkies out there, & lots of them. But after a while, enmeshed in that lifestyle, you start to see narcotics as just another utility. Staying up late, turning to amphetamines like a cup of coffee. On a come down? Hit some weed to take the edge off, just like someone would take aspirin for a headache. You start to look at the world through different eyes, caffeine for breakfast, a dopamine hit of chocolate, the oxytocin of love. We're all unavoidably reliant on chemicals, fats, proteins. The line between drug user & not starts to blur. Alcohol & tobacco are just about the most harmful substances on the planet, our perspective on drugs mostly comes down to politics. & the more closely you look at the world, the more you'll see it like this, made up of arbitrary lines, drawn in the sand. Homosexuality was only legalised in the UK in 1967. In the USA the drinking age is 21, in Austria, Switzerland, & Portugal it's 16. Who is to say what's right & appropriate? But then, that line of argument can be used to excuse whatever kind of inappropriate behaviour you have a predilection for. But to stand on one side of the divide & claim moral superiority, over so-called drug abusers, when you yourself are propped up by chemicals on all sides is sheer hypocrisy.

The underlying question is, what exactly is normal? Because culture shifts, things change, perceptions change. But the point I want to make is deeper than that still, it's that you are no different. Your perceptions are liable to change. & though we might envision ourselves as having a fixed immutable identity, you are in fact in perpetual flux, transforming, evolving. But if you allow yourself to be trapped by misconceptions you can start to rot from the inside. & it will manifest in anti-social behaviour, stress related illnesses, psychological hang-ups. Trust me I've been there! So, here I am, trying to get you to believe in a future that is worth fighting for! Trying to get people to care, because that's what it always comes down to, an expression of love. Reaching for your full potential, for all those who might benefit from your success, those you might inspire to do likewise, those you can help along the way, & for your own well-being! Because when you are properly focused, properly motivated, then you will have the chance to experience what it means to be fully alive. You can start to reach for the elation which is bringing tears to my eyes in this moment. I want to help you believe, in your own ability to change, & in your ability to discover your essence. That which makes you who you truly are! I want you to discover a deeper connection with reality, to let wisdom guide your voice, & to make yourself be heard, by those who so desperately need your help. I want you to turn your pain & frustration into something which makes you proud. I want you to find your talents, &

actively work toward making the world a better place, through love, kindness, & laughter!

But the way to do this is not by distancing yourself from others, it is to make yourself humble, it is to open yourself up to the world. It is to make yourself vulnerable. You have to learn how to take risks, & you have to learn how to trust. To trust in others, to trust in the future, & to trust in yourself. Because when you are not self-loathing, self-sabotaging, twisted, & confused, you will come to find that you are far stronger than you ever believed possible. & if you are no longer afraid to genuinely care, then you will be propelled by an unimaginable force, to achieve your dreams, & to make the impossible a reality! & when you are the one who's getting all the freaky sex, I'll be the one who's clapping from the side lines!

& of course, this is serious, it is quite literally a matter of life & death! This is someone who nearly stepped over the edge into an atrocity of their very own making, reaching out to others, to pull them back from the brink. I need people to hear this, I need this message to spread, & I need the help of anyone who ever reads this, in encouraging other people to read it as well. I need your help, genuinely! But when you are facing the gallows, humour is perhaps the only thing you have left. If this isn't entertaining then why should anybody give a fuck? That's why the conclusion to the Poetry of Chaos is so relentlessly ultra-violent. You want to be entertained, comedy, horror, I'll gladly be your performing monkey if it helps the core message spread. Because I am absolutely convinced that I have this shit figured out, that I know first-hand what you need to understand to take control of your life, to find peace, & joy. Because I've seen first-hand what works, I also understand why it does, & I've broken it all down into simple steps which even a child could understand.

The Optimal Path is exactly what it sounds like, from someone who has turned their autistic obsession toward the discovery of an irrefutable truth. I can see how it all pieces together quite beautifully, like a code that's imprinted into the patterns of sports, story-telling, inter-personal relationships, music. It's all around you, it's what makes reality function in the way that it does, & I have found balance within myself as a result, & an overwhelming love, which spills over whenever I sit down to write. A love, not just for mankind, but for existence itself, to consciousness, to all that is! I feel that palpable connection, right now, with you, as I am writing these words. You are not alone! However, much you self-loathingly want to believe that, you are simply not! & it's not about me as an individual connecting to you as an individual. It's the connection that exists between everything, like a mycelial network, the Tao, the forces beyond our realms of perception, or the incalculable footprint of chaos theory. God, I really did do a lot of drugs in the 90's, & the 00's, & the 10's.

Beyond those things I've come to find the hidden catalyst for action, which I've never heard anybody discuss, in any sphere of psychology. From my own personal form of dramatic abstraction, something which I call 'The Playmaker.' Which is also the title of the 2nd book in 'The Optimal Path' series, which is soon to be released. Without this profound moment of realisation none of these books would exist, & through the journey of discovery which unfolds in the second book we come to the antithesis of the Playmaker, which I call 'The Walled Garden,' which is the title of the 3rd book in the trilogy. I've been a busy bunny, but I'm all about moving forward! Being in the moment, so that's going to be the end of our little retrospective tour. We're moving on to bigger & better things, & now I genuinely don't have the first fucking clue what the rest of this book is going to be about? That's the way we roll baby, winging it from start to finish, flowing with the chaos, trusting to a deeper level of intuition, evolving, expanding, mutating. I swear to fuck you ain't seen nothing like this before! & we're just getting started!

As he slams back a shot of Jack, & follows it up with a swig of coke. A night of drinking, & not giving a fuck! Soon it will all be, shaved head (grade 3.) Ketogenic, intermittent fasting, pull-ups, cardio, & meditation. But tonight, it's 'eat your cake & have it too!' That's right Kaczynski! You pedantic cunt! In the process of true understanding you have to see yourself in the position of those you oppose, even a creature such as the Unabomber. & maybe Ted & I share a certain mistrust, as regards the advancement of technology, & an over exposure to psychedelics. But when you are overwrought with cognition, the mind falls in love with itself, you become focused on your point of obsession, & blind to the alternatives. Like the reasoning behind the holocaust, its abhorrent, ideologies taken to the extreme. Beyond reason, compassion, open awareness, even the acknowledgement of the atrocities you choose to commit.

You have to instead learn how to feel, & that's some seriously scary shit! That's making yourself vulnerable, trusting blindly, & going out on a limb all at the same time. & you might think you are ready to do that, you might tell yourself that you are, but I have rarely in my life ever met someone truly like that! That's the nature of walking the Optimal Path, it's taking responsibility, putting yourself out there, for others to criticise & lambast. It's to make yourself vulnerable to an uncaring world, & to hope beyond hope, that people will appreciate the nature of the endeavour, even if they do not share in your views. & that somehow, you can shed a light on the commonality, which people, these days, so actively try to destroy. Never admitting to themselves, the monsters that they become in the process! Everything that I represent, everything which I have tried to capture in these books is the polar opposite of extremism, the opposite of genocide, & hatred, it is embodied in the virtue of thinking for yourself, & of universal love. But not represented as some abstract ideological theory, but the very fuel behind deep individual, & social transformation. It is the reason for self-nurture, making the right choices, the hard choices, day after day. It's not just something in which to believe, it's something to be acted out, a truth to be lived!

SELFIE

Look at me, am I not gorgeous? Am I not beautiful? Am I not wonderous to behold? Look at me, look at me, look at me!!! Life in a binary world. Short term dopamine feedback loops. Firewalled from reality. A digital native, this is the world into which I was born. My earliest memories were of my parents posting pictures of me online, & the faceless clap machines fuelling my sense of validation. My connection to my mother perverted, corrupted, love by proxy. Now here I am, a slave to the likes. Am I not gorgeous? Am I not beautiful? Smash that like button, tell me, I need to know, am I not wonderous to behold? More beautiful than a sunset? Nobody cares about those pictures, nobody gives a fuck about the things I am really interested in, but my selfies, my glorious selfies, that's how I get all my likes! Encouraged to be self-obsessed. Regressing into self-investment. Personality diminishing. Obsessed solely with appearance. I am in love with myself, the camera is too! Can't you tell? If I hold it at just such an angle, & I pout, & I flutter. It's an art, it takes time, & maybe one day I will capture the perfect selfie. Where are the likes goddamit?!!

You are either my enemy or my friend in this binary world, there is no middle ground here! I was born into a cyberspace where aggression is freely expressed. On platforms with limited text, which encourage the expression of negative emotions, which have literally bred a generation of trolls. It's a toxic environment. This isn't an addiction, it's conditioning, which is far more insidious, far more difficult to reverse. The mass psychosis of social media is all pervasive, it's inescapable. & like an alcoholic, the world has yet to even acknowledge the fact that it has a problem, we're still deeply in the denial phase. & it's not about harmful posts, traumatic imagery, or overuse, your intentions are completely fucking irrelevant, it's the entire structure of the manipulation machine, designed explicitly to addict, to swallow your conscious attention. You are exposed to harm by your very participation. It's the truncated attention span, the emphasis on the expression of unbridled, sharp, primal emotions. It facilitates dehumanisation, hate speech, fake news, cyber-bullying, harassment, stalking, paedophilia. Sold with the promise of connectivity, it has had the polar opposite effect, causing a lack of real-world communication, because it ravenously consumes your time & focus. Attention grabbing, quick stimulation, causing you to dip in frequently, unconsciously, for the pings, the notifications, the group chats. Why is my phone in my hand? Conditioning your brain & central nervous system. Algorithms & networks, catering to human pathology in its most extreme forms. People don't necessarily believe the things that they post, their moral compass doesn't even get a look in, because it's all about provoking a reaction!

& so much of it is about peer control, guilting, social ranking, shaming, bullying, from people who feel insignificant. People who find validation in torturing others, hurting others for their own sense of security, due to their own status anxiety, because they themselves feel lost, & isolated. & their abhorrent actions are wholly in line with the punishment/reward systems on which these networks are founded, to be noticed, or ignored. To be neutral is to be irrelevant, they have been trained to be controversial.

Stupid, slut, cunt, fuck, who does she think she is, stealing my pose!? She knows that's how I do my make-up, look at her with her stupid ugly little teddy bears in the background, eating a banana! She's stealing my shtick, the fucking cow! Well, just you wait & see what I have in store for you, you little bitch. Your world is about to end, you're about to get the online psychological equivalent of a curb stomping! You just fucked with the wrong hoe! I may feel insignificant, disenfranchised, but if I can at least torture you, then I will have agency in the world, it will give me meaning, it will give me status! & it will give me power!

& I personally was not born into a world of mobile phones, let alone social media. I have a works mobile, a dumb phone, that is only ever switched on when I'm on shift. & I've never been a member of any form of online social network in my entire life, because it has always creeped the ever-loving fuck out of me! I'm almost entirely on the outside looking in, but I can see the epidemic exactly for what it is, because I myself have suffered from personality disorders, & that's exactly what social media does, it generates personality disorders, & it's making a religion out of narcissism. The reason I never got onboard with any of it was that I know how badly it would have fucked me up! Because I've got an addictive personality, I'm easily conditioned, I've been ostracised numerous times, why put myself through that inevitability again, the only difference being that this time it's happening online. I was an approval seeking whore back in my late teens, early twenties, a chronic validation seeker, like a junkie looking for a fix, in part because I'd felt socially excluded from such a young age. & here I'm creating the image of an obsessive narcissistic selfie taker, but it's not really to say that I'm any better than that, because I'm so totally fucking not! But adults don't interact with social media in the same way as those who are born into it. Most people don't see the catastrophic implications, partially because they don't want to criticise something which has such utility in their own lives, & also because they simply don't understand it. But this is an age-old problem believe it or not. It's actually something which Lao Tsu teaches about in the Tao De Ching, as does Buddha. If anything, cyberspace is the perfect analogy for what they were teaching. It's possible to find peace & contentment, to be joyous, to become enlightened, but one of the greatest impediments to that is the nature of the human mind.

The mind is a tool, it uses symbolism, dramatic abstraction, various different devices, to stir your imagination, your memory, & it can be used to think creatively, to ensure your safety, to plan for the future. A person with a healthy relationship with their mind & thoughts, appreciates simplicity, they have clarity, they can interpret counter-intuitive wisdom, & quieten their mind at will. They remain in control & do not seek identification with their mind. Who they are is something deeper. They are able to stay fully present. The problem comes when the mind is clouded with anxiety, worrying about the future, self-consciousness dredged up by negative memories, an endless chatter of the mind, obsessive inescapable spiralling loops of thought. A problem exacerbated by alcohol, & addictive behaviours. This internal struggle is as old as mankind. Getting lost in symbolism, losing touch with reality, training yourself to be present for the sake of your loved ones, this was always difficult. But for a generation born into a world of social media? That challenge becomes fucking astronomical!!!!!!! Because it does everything it physically can to break your concentration, to draw out your worst tendencies, to keep you infantilised, & the entire world has yet to switch on to how fucked it is! Because future generations won't even notice the lack of biodiversity, the water wars, or the superstorms, because they'll be eternally lost to cyberspace. This is the true pollutant of the human world, & it is psychological, but it will, given time, manifest in unthinkably destructive realities.

You should kill yourself, You should kill yourself, You should kill yourself, You should kill yourself, You should kill yourself, You should kill yourself, You should kill yourself, You should kill yourself, You should kill yourself, You should kill yourself, You should kill yourself, You should kill yourself, You should kill yourself, etched across a thousand message boards, a million screens. A sentiment which could almost never be expressed in a face to face interaction. But is made possible directly because of the dehumanising nature of the platforms on which it is expressed. Interacting with digital renditions of other people, things, places, events, it's life inside a simulation. It allows you to be callous, unthinking, vile, it fucking encourages it. But the polar opposite is someone who has discovered a clarity of thought, who has learned to care about others, & just for the record, DO NOT FUCKING KILL YOURSELF!!! Do not hurt yourself, or others, especially because of anything I ever write. The whole purpose of this endeavour is to try & get through to those who have never had a chance, to those who don't believe there is anybody out there who cares. There is a depth to reality beyond what the average person experienced before the invention of the mobile phone. & there's certainly a world beyond social media, though for kids brought into this world any break from their smartphone is merely a hiatus, from the unbounded accessibility. A week detoxing offline, merely a pause for breath in a lifetime consumed by social media conglomerates. & when you are not online, you're still not really there, it's got a grip of you, you struggle to make genuine connections. It's not even that it distorts your perception of reality, it envelops it. & the skyrocketing teen suicide & eating disorders, are just early indicators, it fails to capture the everyday subtle implications on the global psyche, the depression, & anxiety. Don't underestimate the effects of psychological, & emotional violence, I'd rather take a knife attack in a graveyard any day of the week!

Everything is broken down into headlines, & taken out of context. You are always under surveillance. & if a joke gets misconstrued, then the mob will descend, your livelihood will be taken from you, your very life in jeopardy. It's a game with the most serious of consequences! & given the nature of the shared delusion, how are kids born into it, who are completely oblivious to the behaviour modification, the malicious manipulation, ever going to be able to extricate themselves from it, they'll never have known anything else. & they can't look for help without being labelled an attention seeker. Trapped in a self-perpetuating loop of a system intrinsically designed to provoke feelings of confrontation, resentment, hatred, anger, aggression, specifically to keep your attention focused on social media, with no countervailing influences, nothing to burst the bubble. A generation raised with a technologically induced psychotic disorder, amongst a whole host of other psychiatric problems. But let's just focus on one for now, shall we? & don't let me give you the impression that I am an expert, as I am genuinely learning as I go.

6 out of every 10 posts are selfies, because they generate likes. People are being conditioned to focus on themselves, & as children that's how we start out in life, but as we mature our focus is externalised, we learn to care about others. In this sense making people fixated on their personal appearance, making them completely self-involved is highly regressive, & psychologically damaging. Narcissism is in itself a defence mechanism, & here are some of the destructive behaviours which a narcissist tends to display. Denial, devaluation, displacement, dissociation, fantasy, isolation of effect, fantasies of omnipotence, projection, rationalisation, cognitive dissonance, reaction formation, repression, & splitting. I've personally experienced most of these first hand, having exhibited them to devastating effect in my own personal life, & been the victim of other people's splitting, reaction formation, etc. What I'm saying is that I may not have a doctorate but I know the view from the trenches, all too well, unfortunately.

(Warning: This next chunk, a description of individual defence mechanisms, is rather technical.)

Denial is when people ignore unpleasant facts, filter out data & content which contravene their self-image. It's common to see little echo-chambers online, people feeding off one another to create fractious little groups?

Devaluation, attributing negative qualities to others, or to yourself. Designed to mitigate the importance of an individual. How cheaply terms such as alt-right, snowflake, trans-phobic, racist, are thrown around these days? & once you've labelled a person then anything that they have to say is no longer relevant. Because of course everything falls into the binary perspective of good guy, bad guy. When the self is devalued its self-destructive, this ties in with splitting. An example of which is the inability to psychologically integrate complex opposing characteristics of another person, envisioning them as two separate things, one good, one bad. Like a child relating to their mother as an idealised perfection. Oscillating between displays of adoration, & horrific tantrums. When splitting is turned on the self, the narcissist creates a perfect ideal of themselves & when they fail to live up to it, they strongly chastise & devalue themselves, as less than worthless.

My little image there of the angry narcissist, cyber-bullying the girl with the banana & teddy bears is an example of displacement. When we cannot control the resources of our frustration, pain, envy, we tend to pick a fight with someone who seems weaker, those who are perceived as less menacing. Like kids who can't deal with parental conflict going out to bully others.

Dissociation is losing track of space & time, shutting out incoming information & circumstances. This ties in with multiple-personality disorders, something which I seemed to exhibit when I was drinking. My friends wanted to videotape me & play me back to myself, like they were dealing with a completely different person, apparently even the way I moved was different. All I would get were little flashes of memory, it was highly addictive & ultimately self-defeating.

Fantasy as a central means to deal with conflict is pathological, narcissists have grandiose fantasies which are incommensurate with their accomplishments & abilities. I'm still harbouring the fantasy of being a successful writer, all evidence to the contrary, I wouldn't even be doing this without that particular fantasy. Fantasies can also be imbued on others, & I'm not even going to get in to the problems I've had with that one!

Isolation of effect, when cognition is divorced from emotion, it's basically going numb, been there, got the t-shirt! It can have uses in short term trauma but when this becomes habitual it becomes pathological.

Omnipotence, when you think of yourself as powerful, intelligent, influential, not an affectation but an ingrained inner conviction which borders on magical thinking, but maybe one day everyone will buy my books! I'm going to be a star! He says, fending off inadequacies & limitations.

Projection, putting onto others the uncomfortable feelings & traits which we ourselves possess, such as the misplaced homophobia projected at me which I mentioned in the last chapter. Or perhaps that was a reaction formation, from a closeted homosexual, expressing diametrically opposed convictions, to contain & avoid having to face up to uncomfortable truths about themselves. But in terms of projection, we disown these discordant features, & preserve the right to criticise others for having or displaying them. People rarely know they are doing it; they explain away projection as their reaction to the behaviour of others. This reminds me of the Stockwell strangler Kenneth Erskine, & other serial killers who prey on prostitutes. They believe that they are doing it because these girls are promiscuous & immoral, but it's really traits within themselves that they have projected onto their victims. & you could chalk that up as a rationalisation, to cast one's behaviour after the fact in a favourable light, to justify one's misconduct.

& then there's good old repression, the removal from consciousness of forbidden thoughts & wishes. Which tend to ferment in the unconscious, in turn creating yet more defence mechanisms, & I have novels still yet to be written on the subject of repressed emotion, so I won't go into that here. Then there's also cognitive dissonance, devaluing that which we cannot attain. & you can see that with celebrity culture these days, 'fit shaming' I believe they call it. & undoing, which is the attempt to take back an unconscious behaviour or thought that is unacceptable or hurtful.

Narcissism, like autism is a spectrum, we are all narcissistic to some degree. Most of my experiences seem to revolve around extended periods, like manic bipolar episodes, in my early twenties, when I was drinking heavily, taking a lot of drugs, surrounded by large crowds. There's what's described as malignant narcissism, which describes people without empathy, often exploitative, abusive, & mired in criminal behaviour, & thankfully I'm not at that end of the spectrum. But I've been through phases where I was addicted to validation, & it's like I've tried out every psychological coping strategy, or defence mechanism you can think of, at one time or another, just so that I could bury my emotions. But I have come under emotional attack from some extreme narcissists throughout my life, both male & female. Often in inescapable environments, like school or work, the high school jocks, A-crowd super bitches, mini-Hitler managers, meat-head bouncers, you name it. & the number one trick in the arsenal always seems to be devaluing, putting you down, attacking your status. & when I was a vulnerable little kid, I took it very seriously to heart, & because I was ostracised as a child, I would self-sabotage later in life, pushing people away, so that the world was rendered familiar, so that I was perpetually excluded. Then along came social media, & stole the world away, saving me the hassle. I might as well have ceased to exist, because I refused to play the game. But now I'm sitting on the outside looking at the way that people are generally behaving in society, & ticking the boxes of my own personality disorders, learning about myself in the process. & though you might dismiss me as a doomsayer, like the cheeseboard wearers of yesteryear, let me spell it out to you in no uncertain terms. In our current state, we are walking blindfold into a nightmare of catastrophic proportions! In a narcissistic society those who do not have, get less & less, those who do have, take more & more, without thought for the consequences. & throughout history such societies always explode, have always led to massive wars, bloody rebellion, tens of millions dead. Finally, the losers take to arms, ruin the wealth & drive civilisation back a hundred years, it's an ongoing cycle. But something radically new & terrifying has happened, narcissism has become its own religion, a malicious, toxic, cult.

The narcissistic response to trauma, to avoid a sense of vulnerability, is to create a false self, an idealised projection, a fantasy of omnipotence, & extreme self-importance. We think of narcissists as having extremely large egos but that's not true, that's not how it works. This is often something which happens in childhood, as a response to abuse, but the narcissist chooses to make a sacrifice, in paganistic worship to this false self, this god-like persona they have created, & the sacrifice is their true self. & the frustration which those who are close to the narcissist experience is that when they try to penetrate beneath the exterior, they will find there is nothing there, just a void. & the narcissist requires constant validation to sustain the fantasy of the false self which they have created.

The dominant metaphor in our culture is the network, it's how we envision society, computers, business, marketing, commuting infrastructure, the human brain. Every narcissist is a one-man cult, networking on a global scale, with as many gods as worshippers. & the inner conflict of the narcissist invariably leads to aggression, the same psychopathic desire to eradicate weakness as the Stockwell strangler, loathing their own fragility, instability, lashing out at the world as a projection of self-hatred. & what underpins the entire of social media is the craving to be heard, to be seen, but all you get is a simulated interaction, which promises but never delivers! But as Malcolm Tucker says, 'it's not my fucking problem!' I've already been through all of this, & sorted my shit out, the rest of you guys don't even know what you're in for, & it isn't pleasant I can assure you of that!

What is the internet to me? It's a utility, with free music, free videos, which I am admittedly addicted to. A source of free information, maps, etc. But it's not a leash, & you can shove your smartphone up your arse. I don't even have a ringer on my landline, that's right, you can all fuck off with your double glazing, life insurance, & what have you's. & it deeply concerns me that I may one day have to use social media to market these books, something which I'm trying to avoid at all costs. & why should I even be sat here writing all of this? It's because I'm not self-obsessed, regressing into a world of selfies! It's because I do care about the world & what happens to people, other than myself. What really is the point of having gone through all the shit that I have, if it can't at least be used to help others who are going through something similar. & wouldn't you know? It turns out that the entire fucking world, below the age of twenty, give or take, & generations yet still to be born, are all going through something extremely fucking similar! It seems like dealing with psychological torment is a growth industry, & I could probably make a tidy little wage, as a counsellor working on a one to one basis. But when there's an epidemic of global proportions you've got to try & reach out to as many people as possible, so that's why I'm here, that's why I'm writing. Because I'm choosing to make it my problem, the self-harm, the suicides, the active shooters, I'm putting the responsibility on my shoulders, to talk to an entire fucking planet. If ever there was a more ironically narcissistic endeavour? I want to change the fate of mankind! There's your grandiose fantasy for you! But it's not even really about that, it's about getting through to one person, it's about getting through to you in this moment. Trying to give you just a glimpse of what true intimacy really means, because I genuinely want you to feel that this was written for you, to you, because once again the tears are streaming down my face, & even if the entire world doesn't care, I do, I genuinely do!

From my years working on suicide lines, it only ever felt like we were skimming across an ocean. I've had my eyes opened to real pain & hardships. I've worked with people with physical & mental disabilities, who daily live through unfathomable distress. & it seems like so much of the pain in our society could be so easily avoided, if we weren't so afraid to express ourselves. So that's part of what I'm trying to do here, expressing myself in a way that you are unlikely to ever have seen anywhere else. I want to show people the importance of carving out your own sense of purpose, & why you should put caring about others at the top of your priorities. & help give you just a little basic guidance on how to deal with your emotions. & above all, to give a message of hope to those who believe they are beyond redemption, who believe the whole world is ignoring them, & that there's no way out of their existential torment. Because I didn't know if it could be done, I couldn't see it, I couldn't envision a possible future. & fuck knows how I survived, through the years of suicidal ideation, to deliver this message, but I did it, I found peace, & more! I found a world that was always trapped behind symbolism. I let go of my attempts to conceptualise existence with the cognitive mind, & I simply opened my awareness. I used to envision myself a god, I was lost in the false self, but I let go of the fantasy. I began to discover my true self, flawed, & vulnerable, & the more I embraced it the less anxious I became. & over time, through self-analysis I shed off one neurotic tendency after another. I trained my mind to be calm. I learned to be appreciative of the simplest things. I set myself free in a way that I could never have envisioned, because trapped inside myself I couldn't begin to imagine the depth & complexity of the world that lay beyond the illusion I had created for myself.

Full disclaimer! This piece of prose was heavily inspired by the videos of Richard Grannon & the psychiatrist Sam Vaknin. But this rejumbling of ideas is my own creation, & as such is not intended to directly express anybody else's views. But in truth my interest lies far away from social media, in the ancient texts of the Taoist masters. This isn't about freeing yourself from a digital trap, it's about a deeper connection to reality & awareness. If we allow ourselves to be consumed by the world, we cannot see it for what it is. My interest is in discovering my true nature, & expressing it clearly. My interest is in finding how opposing forces complement one another, not in creating division, political or otherwise! My interest is in seeking balance, in all things, reason, wisdom, & joy. My intention is to challenge your perceptions, & to show love, to those who need it most! Or maybe it's all one massive, hollow, attention seeking scam? Subconsciously designed to fuel my narcissistic tendencies? I'll let you decide.

STREET-GOTH

In the centre of Glasgow there is a pedestrian zone. A few blocks up, & running parallel to the River Clyde, is Argyll Street, & the St Enoch's Centre. At a right angle, running directly up through town is Buchanan Street, & the Buchanan Galleries. At the top it curls round to the left, past the steps of the Royal Concert Hall, & turns into Sauchiehall Street. Branching off the middle of Buchanan Street, to the left is Gordon Street, leading down to Central Station. & to the right, leading in the direction of George Square, & Queen Street station, is the Gallery of Modern Art. You may know it from the statue of the Duke of Wellington, the cunt with a traffic cone for a hat, in front of those vast Corinthian pillars. Around the steps of which the swarms of unruly goths, & skateboarders used to coalesce. The type of miscreants who could be found drinking in graveyards. They were out there on the city streets, day & night, with the neds & the junkies, chasing after drugs, with the ever-present threat of violence all around them. But in the end, the core group disbanded after one of them was stabbed to death. During those times I was always hanging around in town, these days it's usually just something I pass through on the way to work.

The wee guy who sold the Big Issue up on Buchanan Street got murdered recently as well, or so I heard. 'Don't be shy, give it a try,' he would shout, with gusto. The black guy who used to play the guitar up on Sauchiehall street was run off by racist cunts, the video was online a few years back. Both the ABC, & Victoria's nightclub have gone up in flames, the Art School too, twice, it seems like we have a firebug in our midst. Or perhaps in some cases it's what the racist cunts might call 'Jewish Lightning' (he says, trying to distance himself from the irresistibly colourful phrase,) insurance fraud, as the storefront businesses crumble? They say there are shops on the high street which can't financially support their own existence. & the only reason the business puts on this hollow front is to maintain a façade for the sake of online sales. & up on Sauchiehall Street the charity muggers have created an impenetrable minefield, between Poundland & KFC, it's Kentucky Fried Chuggers, as far as the eye can see. On the next block up is where the fire at Victoria's happened, & the building's completely gone. It looks like a pirate's grin, with a missing tooth. I suppose it just about sums the place up these days, it looks like a town that's had the shit kicked out of it. & it's always a tragedy when one of these old buildings goes up in flames, because what are they going to replace it with? A featureless dull, Lego brick, rectangle. & the sleepover is getting out of hand, doorways filled with sleeping bags, it's not far off a tent city these days.

You can't smile in this place, for fear of someone running up & trying to sell you something. & I'll not lie to you, I was one of those kids, in the smart suit, with the big grin. Trying to flog haircuts, with a studio photoshoot. Don't be narcissistic he says, out of one side of his mouth, while trying to profit off the vanity of others. Those intrusive cold callers I myself despise, I was one of those too, for over a decade. There's nothing I haven't sold at one time or another, mobile phones, gas suppliers, time share, dignity, my soul. In one job I used to have this spiel, 'Hi, I'm calling from the national survey centre, & I was wondering if you could take a moment to answer a few…' 9 to 5, day after day, week after week, 'Hi, I'm calling from the national survey centre, & I was wondering if you could take a moment to answer a few…' Quite literally, seeping into your nightmares. The national survey centre? Some made up bullshit, preying upon people's good nature, so that we could ask them about their insurance, & double glazing, weeding out potential victims for the hard-sell which would inevitably follow. I do have a lovely telephone voice, when I put my mind to it, posh & friendly, doodling cartoons about call centre related suicide at the same time. & on this one call, I start off by saying, 'Hi, I'm calling from the national survey centre, & I was wondering if you could take a moment to...' & I hear a click on the other end of the phone, which I assume is the lady on the other end hanging up on me. So, I say, 'Hi, I'm calling from the national survey centre, & I was wondering if you could take a moment... (click) ...to kiss my fucking ass!!' But there must have been two people who picked up the phone, & the click I heard was the 2nd person hanging up their receiver. & I'll never forget the palpable shock & horror of the 'ooohhh??' noise which the lady made on the other end of the phone. Didn't hang around for an apology, hung up on reflex, moved on to the next call, hoping there weren't going to be dire repercussions.

Horrendous places, call centres! Put your hand up to go for a piss, automated dialling systems so that you are never not on a call. It's constant, like factory work, but you're not using your hands, it's just your voice, the constant, inescapable repetition, it's fucking brain damage! & one time, me & my ex, were working at a place which had a sweepstake at the first of the month. You could pick up near a thousand pound if you were the first to hit all the targets. & we went in & blitzed it, between the two of us, but made the mistake of turning up late the following day, so both got summarily fired so they didn't have to fork out. & when we called in, the smug mini-Hitler in the office created a firewall so that we couldn't claim what we'd worked for. But the joke was on her because the following month the boss fucked off to the Algarve without paying anybody's wages. We got out at the right time, missing out on a bonus is one thing, but a month's wages? They are all run by wankers these businesses, & fly by night is standard operating procedure. But person to person is tough, especially because you're working purely for commission. In the place I worked last, the brain washing was next level. In the morning there were motivational speeches, with the boss handing out mini cash prizes, standing around in a circle, high fiving each other. Everything was about positivity, nothing negative, or anything that could be construed as negative, only success dare be spoken. & then I heard about what had happened the week before I turned up. Everybody standing in their circle, first thing in the morning, are told to close their eyes. If you feel a tap on the shoulder, take your belongings & fuck off! No talking, just take your shit, & walk! Labour laws, who needs them?

But there are other reasons to repress a smile, it's wall to wall with unfortunate people, in genuine trouble. Homeless, & beggars, a high percentage of which are Eastern European. & I'm not complaining, like... look at this shabby lot, lowering the tone? Because, what kind of a self-important cunt thinks like that? & can't empathise with those in such difficult circumstances? & besides, I'm as shabby as the rest of them. But it seems inappropriate to smile, when people are sitting up on their knees in true, old school, supplication, paper cup outstretched, head bowed. It seems that solemnity is the only appropriate conduct in these circumstances. & right in that chokepoint of chuggers between KFC & the Halifax, dire prognostications are being bellowed, through a loud speaker. It's all sinners & hellfire, deep throated evangelical beliefs, the kind one only tends to hear through a megaphone. Further up the street the black guitarist has been replaced by a violinist, playing a piece that one might hear on the streets of Kabul. The problem is there's only one verse, which he plays over & over indefinitely, & don't get too close, or he'll want to shake your hand, his grin is more toothless than the aforementioned pirate, & once he's got you then you'll feel compelled to pay out. & old school supplication isn't for everyone, the Scots are taking a more pro-active approach these days, they'll come right up bold as brass. You can give them your coppers, & they will literally hand them right back to you, it's folding money they are after, let's take a walk up to the bank machine. & you'll see them all sitting in corners spiced out their nut, fast asleep & drooling. Spice is a new thing, you smoke it like cannabis, but it's nothing like it. From those I know that have tried it, the sensations are horrible. Unlike most recreational drugs, there is no upside, no pleasurable kick to be had. But it makes you numb, numb to the cold, it means you can handle the elements, it's cheap, & it knocks you the fuck out, ideal for those who are sleeping rough. Well, it beats the krokodil anyway!

But I'd be remiss if I weren't to explain how gentrified the place has become. In such a very short space of time, like the Pollock centre, or the cobbled streets in the Poetry of Chaos, 'hipsters exchanging home-made candles,' the effect has spread across the entire city. & I look at these smartly turned out kids, walking about at night, like they don't even know how dangerous this place is. But is it really as dangerous as I remember, or has that gone too, passed like the drizzle of my youth? Has social media made the streets a safer place? Do we have that to thank it for? Are the kids too busy updating their profiles, to be out engaging in some good old-fashioned ultra-violence? But in truth I tend to look right past the pedestrians, at a most wonderful spectacle, the city pigeons! Turning, & swooping in unison, over, round, & through the streets. Jumping off high ledges in ones & twos, stragglers bringing up the rear. On occasion, you'll see one holding their wings in a tight V shape, a specialisation I've only ever noticed in pigeons. & up above, at a higher stratum, are gulls gliding with their wings in an M shape, most likely from the large quantity of McDonalds they've consumed. Scavengers both, don't let them see you with a sausage roll in your hands, or you'll be in trouble. I'm less interested in them on the ground, it's in the air that they are astonishing to me, it's flight that fascinates me. Not that I know the first thing about aviation, or aerodynamics, but I can imagine what it would be like to fly. & while others might be keeping up with the Jones's, or competing to outdo one another on social media, with my head so firmly in the clouds, my jealousy is reserved for the crows, & the filthy, club-footed, city pigeons.

When I'm talking about the Taoist masters I'm not talking about an intellectual fascination, signposting my spirituality, or some such nonsense. I'm talking about a skillset, something to be practiced, as a way of being. Part of which is present moment awareness, something which very few people actively employ on a daily basis. It's not just meditation, though meditation helps calm the mind, lessens the fluctuating egoic impulses. I'm talking about being present in the world, paying close attention, really listening when others talk, noticing the seemingly inconsequential details, letting yourself breathe. Not allowing yourself to be overwhelmed by the complexity of your own life, at peace within yourself. Not distracted by compulsive thought, not trying to escape into your imagination, experiencing existence as it unfolds around you. I was on the bus to work the other day, & nobody on that bus will remember that journey, for it was wholly unremarkable. The wind was strong enough to shiver the grass. Specks of rain gathering on the fogged windowpane. A flight of sparrows passes overhead, the evergreens blustering. I hear the ping of a mobile phone. We pass a cluster of workmen in yellow jackets. A Scotland flag is wrapped tightly round a flag pole. Strings of fluorescent orange tape stream out from a broken bus shelter. & one at a time a team of gulls comes into view, & not a flap amongst them, a testament to the strength of the wind. As we burl around a procession of roundabouts. The specks on the windowpane turn into a mask of rivulets, & I am lightly showered from the spray of an open window. I find it pleasant, like the spindrift of a distant boat ride, I recall my sunburn & blistered feet. This boat, my saviour, days of arduous walking over, going home. Yesterday it was clothes on the radiator, & a hot shower, a proper soaking, so this is nothing! A luminous green bag flutters on a barbed wire fence. The trash lends a bit of colour to these drab grey streets. & as I sit to write these words, on a long metal bench, in the bus station, a chap with learning difficulties, in a wheelchair, reaches out to me, making low-pitched croaks from the back of his throat. Bent on one side to get a good look at me, with a broad smile, which I return. I stop momentarily under a heater as a man in a grey bunnet sits passively staring out into the rain. Bright yellow buckets capture leaks from the roof in the town centre. Welcome to Cumbernauld.

& though you might think this is all so vapid & dreich, these little foibles, the burned-out buildings, the dirty pigeons, to me those are the best bits, the underlying character of the world. The more attention you place on it, the more fascinating it all becomes, & you will see beauty, & humour where others see none. You will see love in care worn faces, & you will start to see traits you recognise in yourself, reflected back in others. & one of the clearest, & most obvious examples of this sense of connection, is in the flight of birds. I focus on my own reaction, my own feelings as I watch them, & the sensation is like a roller-coaster. I can feel it in the pit of my stomach, at times an almost panicked shortness of breath, as they fly between obstacles. It's a strong visceral feeling, & to see a huge flight of pigeons descending on mass, under wires, round lamp posts, over cars, skimming over the top of crowds on a busy city street, is an overwhelmingly joyous experience. & yes, I'm smiling, in this mausoleum, I can barely contain it. The same is true of rivers, viewed with deep conscious attention, the way they turn, how the water flows, it's mesmeric. It becomes an extension of self; you can feel it as though it were a part of you. I love anything which shows the wind, the unseen forces that surround us, laughing at the little eddies in autumnal leaves. & I'm not trying to force others into my way of thinking, you won't find me marching the streets with a megaphone in hand. But if I've discovered a quiet peace, & contentment, I won't just sit in silence while others are suffering. But the issue is like any addiction, do you really want to change? Are you willing to give up ten minutes a day to start meditating? Most people are not willing to make even the slightest concession. & I'd no sooner force it upon you, than I would knock off the Duke of Wellington's lovely hat. But then, I don't have to put up with you, your anxiety, depression, fluctuating mood swings, it's not my fucking problem. But I would like to help, if I could. I would like to help you be present, for others, & for yourself. I would like to help you build positive daily habits. I would like to help you see things objectively. I would like to help you be in touch with your emotions, & to help you balance them. I would like to help you find self-belief, & purpose. I would like to help you appreciate the little details. & I genuinely do wish peace & joy upon you, but that's something which you need to work toward, something which you have to cultivate. Finding your essence, your true self, can take many years, a lot of introspection, & courage. But there is no greater endeavour, or more rewarding a task which you will ever undertake. Like a bird in flight, it is to be truly set free!

& the problem always starts when we try to overcomplicate things. It's in our psychological defence mechanisms, our attempts to unravel the cosmos which lead to existential depression, the attempts to create a false self for whatever reason. The first task is always to find stillness, to slow down physically, & mentally. We often don't even realise that we're trapped in a cognitive distortion, our minds filtering out all the negative thoughts, & after many years of meditation I still find myself momentarily wrapped up in embarrassments, & regrets. There always seems to be a deeper truth that can be extracted, lessons to be learned from these things. Writing the last chapter was quite eye opening for me, it joins the dots of the god-like narcissistic fantasies of my late teens, & early twenties. It's like little parts of me were trapped until I came to a deeper realisation of the processes which had generated the complications in the first place. Piece by piece I'm winning control over my own psyche, & these arc all common issues which I see daily in the lives of everyone around me, whether they are aware of it or not. But it's difficult to tell a person their flaws, it can be taken as aggression, so instead I've taken to telling the world about mine. & if they feel so inclined, they can take note, & act to set themselves free of anxieties, as I have. Because, over the years, I could give you the answers to all the psychological issues you've ever had, but it would be pointless if you didn't take it on board, or try to contextualise what it might mean in your own life. As such, I see these books as being interactive, it's not just me telling you silly stories, it's supposed to be impactful, it just depends how much you are willing to engage. & I'm not claiming to be infallible, far from it, start off by questioning everything, but try to find the objective truth, don't just rely on opinion. That goes for religious dogma, ideologies, all that stuff, don't let anybody brainwash you, especially not some shabby old street-goth, writing under a pseudonym.

I come out of Buchanan Street bus station, & turn right on West Nile, onto Sauchiehall street, a pair of gulls wheel, screeching high above. I see a lady selling CBD oils out of a red Tardis, with a cycle rack out the back. I pull out my notepad & move out of the way of the cutting wind. Standing at the wall between Bella Vita, & Specsavers, the skyline is dominated by the towering presence of Cineworld. It's dry under foot, with only one big puddle in the middle of the street. It's a brighter day today, but it's still early February, & evidently the low glaring sun is fooling no one, with plenty of beanie's, & bobble hats on display. The seats outside the Italian restaurant sit empty. I would never be caught wearing a bobble hat, not that there's anything wrong with it, it's just not for me. Pigeons clustered on barren trees, & gathered on the glass awning over my head. It's a chugger free zone today, & I'm nursing a sniffle. My nose is doing the suddenly unbearable itchy thing, oh my god, blow my nose, blow my nose, blow my nose! I smell nothing. Pedestrians mostly keeping a uniform pace, going nowhere quickly. A cyclist swerves between benches, & there's a continual hammering of construction noises on all sides. Buses dominate the perpetual hum of traffic. & further up the street there is a blue netting, over the scaffolding, on the building next to the gap that was Victoria's. At street level there is a long mural of kittens playing with yarn. Don't look at the hole, the fire damage, the destruction, look at the kittens, look at the kittens. & I'm reminded of the Clutha bar, a dingy old man's drinking pub, presented by the media as a most treasured landmark, after a helicopter crashed into it. & may they all rest in peace, the old men, the pilots, the big issue vendors, & the dead goths. But I've always been sceptical of the way people respond to tragedy, the enforced silence it creates, & the way people choose to fill the void.

The noise of bagpipes floats up from Buchanan street, & my eye is drawn to three separate people with purple hair, one guy, two girls, the colour of thistles & heather. A man with no leg's zips past on an electric wheelchair, talking into his phone. Why this place I wonder to myself, why have I chosen to describe this exact location? Does this represent the heart of the city to me? I suppose Buchanan Street is mostly an upward slope, whereas this is nice & flat, & I rarely have business on Argyll Street, except for picking up cheap trainers on occasion. It always felt like a walled garden of sorts, this pedestrian zone, when I was out on the streets all the time. Like a game, which children play, where you're not allowed to touch the floor, a little island, of sorts. Constantly making that loop around from Royal Exchange Square to Central Station, either looking for trouble, or running from it. & here I'm stood with a notepad, evidently planning to rob the Bank of Scotland across the street. Or a terrorist perhaps? Taking notes, who does that? I draw the occasional glare; nobody trusts a guy with a notepad. The pigeons are waiting, this is the feeding spot, amongst the stone block benches, maybe that's why this is the place? Maybe I'm an overgrown city pigeon at heart, returning once again, drawn by homing instinct.

Sitting almost directly across the street there is a homeless lady with a paper cup, she has the look of a traditional gypsy. I don't even know if that is an offensive description, I assume everything is these days, though I certainly mean no offense by it. She has dark skin, wizened features, a shawl over her head. I imagine she personally would take more offense to the remark about her wizened features. I start a little, in surprise, as a woman walks past on my blindside, suddenly talking very loudly into her mobile phone. Half of everyone has a phone in their hand, but of those under 50 the percentage is far higher. & piece by piece I'm gradually opening my awareness to more & more of what is going on around me. I realise, all the kids are at school. It's a Tuesday afternoon, yet the moon is still high over the Buchanan Centre, to my right. The pigeons are fluttering around the white rooftop of Lauders across the street, to my left, behind which is the hole, the kittens, & the blue netting. The streets are quite clean, though speckled with gum, a man passes me slurping through a straw. I notice the occasional goth type, & long-haired rockers in leather jackets. I catch the gypsy lady staring at me from across the street, she looks away. She evidently knows this street better than I do, & as per usual I'm the odd one out! Litter pickers pass in fluorescent yellow jackets, causing me to notice another workman on the rooftop across the street. A barking dog sets off the pigeons, straining at his leash.

One of the largest cultural differences amongst the pedestrians, from when I was a kid, is that there are noticeably more oriental people, of all ages. Glasgow is just generally becoming more cosmopolitan as the years go by. A cyclist speeds past with no hands, everyone wears a helmet these days, it seems health & safety has embedded itself in our culture. A little girl throws crumbs for the pigeons, & her mother has two birds on her arms. The little girl shrieks in delight & all the pigeons take flight, but quickly return. A smoker coughs, & I notice that there have been relatively few smokers on display, yet more social change. The loudest noise from this whole scene comes from the clattering of wheels from a hooded skateboarder, who contradictorily is wearing a camouflage jacket. Another cyclist passes through the pigeons, but they take no notice, loud noises seem to be their trigger. A pair of junkies with wicked grins pass close by me, her in a dishevelled pink jacket with a fur-lined hood, blue plastic bag dangling, cigarette in hand, him in a dark navy-blue tracksuit. I seem to be mostly invisible out here, everyone too self-involved to really take notice of anything. A woman with a plastic grin stops a pair of girls, so that a man can take their picture. I overhear that they are journalists. They go on to take a picture of a guy in a white jacket, I don't know, or care why. It all adds to the randomness of events on these city streets. A woman pushes a lady along in a wheelchair (perhaps her mother,) who reminds me of Dame Maggie Smith, wearing a neck brace. Behind them a bow-legged old man, helped along by his wife (I presume,) stops with a hand against the free Wi-Fi station, that's probably as much utility as he could find for the thing anyway. In this moment I count four walking sticks; & I think that the old timer could probably do with one himself. An empty rickshaw slowly passes by, even better, but they don't stop it. & all this time, across the street, along from the gypsy lady, a man has been painting, & selling cartoon pictures of Deadpool. & I've failed to notice it, because there's just too much going on! The wind blows a pigeon feather past my feet, & I put my notepad away, so that I can focus on the birds. The bagpipes never cease!

CONFIDENCE

Back when I was in my teens, I took an interest in the guitar. I had no real aspirations to become a musician. & now that I think about it, I'm starting to question the underlying motivations? & just like most teens who pick up the guitar, perhaps not even realising it, the ultimate goal is invariably to try & lose your virginity. It's simple teen maths, rock star = sex. Except there was, in my case, a rather more direct reason. My closest friend & I seemed to draw the A-crowd rejects, the ones who were a little too unhinged, who had trouble at home, & pushed things too far. Pissing everybody off by stealing girlfriends, being too wild, or excessive. It made for an interesting group but without any girls, it was a bit of a sausage-fest, but for years we were too busy getting wasted, & playing football, to care. But the kids who hung about in the music corridor were a diverse group, well, maybe not diverse exactly, in that they were all nerds, but there were girls, which was a step in the right direction. In the beginning I was probably using the guitar as a disguise, an excuse to hang around the music corridor at lunch time. But soon it wasn't about the girls anymore, they faded into the background, once I started getting into the guitar.

I got a cheap Fender knock off, 'Star Force,' white, & a little Marshall amp, for my birthday. The kids at my school usually had all sorts of stuff that I didn't. At my primary school most of the children lived in schemes, which have since been torn down. With stories of children finding their heroin addicted mothers after they'd hanged themselves, but my secondary school? Some of their folks were millionaires, indoor pools, that kind of shit. Changing schools, I was suddenly exposed to these two polar extremes. Others were kids of divorce, parents rarely around, buying their affection. I'd be lying if I wasn't a little mesmerised by all their gadgets at times. I'd go over to their houses, & get obsessed with games consoles that they'd already outgrown. I had a friend who had all the professional kit, multi-effects pedals, & I was over at his house every other day, the pair of us taking turns at mangling Rage Against the Machine songs, in between horror flicks. I was an intro specialist, I only ever got about a minute into a song before losing interest, & trying to learn something new. At school there was this one kid who started playing at around the same time as me. & it was all about Metallica, those intricate Spanish guitar intros, but after what felt like just a couple of weeks, this fucker is up on stage in front of the entire school nailing the solos as well. He made staggeringly difficult things seem childishly easy. & I hit a wall, never really able to play for more than a few seconds without making some kind of error. But I never really wanted to be a guitarist, so fuck it, doesn't matter, it's not like I care (sniff, sniff.) & eventually I managed to get laid, & the guitar had nothing to do with it. & somewhere, over twenty years later, rotting at the back of a cupboard with its guts hanging out, obscured by dusty VHS cassettes is that same old guitar.

But I was thinking to myself, that guy actually did go on to be a professional guitarist. So maybe the rest of us mere mortals just have to plod away at it, till it finally sinks in. So, I thought I'd give it another shot, & last Christmas my folks got me an acoustic, & I've been plucking away at the thing ever since. But instead of just learning a bunch of intros I focused on one or two songs. The main one was written by Michael Pitt, & it features in a Gus Van Sant film called 'Last Days.' It's called 'From Death to Birth.' I'm a genuine cinephile, with an honour's degree in filmmaking & scriptwriting. I like a wide variety of stuff, from obscure animation, arthouse, black & white foreign cinema, as well as the major blockbusters that everybody else watches. & can say without any reservations that it is my favourite film of all time, & I find it hard to imagine that there will ever be anything that surpasses it. & chances are you probably wouldn't like it, there's barely any dialogue, it's a strange little film, about a musician ghosting around in an old country house, in the days leading up to his suicide. It speaks to a very particular time in my life, & after watching it, I'm quite content to put it right back on from the start. I didn't tell anybody about this film for over two years, & I was travelling daily back & forth to film school at the time, on hour long train journeys with other students, & all we did was talk continuously about movies. I didn't tell anybody because I didn't want to be exposed to their opinions on it. It was too personal to me, & I just didn't want to hear it!

As acoustic guitar songs go, it's not particularly difficult to play, but I just concentrated on that one song. Not even the most intricate parts of it, just enough so that I could comfortably play along from start to finish. I'd pick up the guitar every couple of days, & play it through repeatedly. Till I could make mistakes without being thrown out of rhythm, till I could play it with my eyes closed. Till I got bored & started to mess about, to the point where now I can use the scale & rhythm to improvise riffs which you wouldn't know weren't part of the original song. & yesterday something strange happened. I've never been able to so much as hum along while I was playing the guitar, forget about singing! Well, yesterday I decided to concentrate solely on singing the chorus, 'It's a long, lonely journey from death to birth.' & I just did it over & over, till the key words just seemed to synch up with chord changes in my mind. & by the end of the night I was playing & singing the entire song from beginning to end. & I'm sitting here typing with sore fingers because I've become absolutely obsessed. I'm sitting here writing all of this so that I don't pick up the guitar again, because my fingers are blistered. Not only that but I've just scarfed back a packet of wine gums, it's very much comfort eating, & avoidance!

When I was in my early twenties, I decided to start a band, with me as the lead singer. We had a lead guitarist, rhythm, bass, drums. & they were all proper musicians, unlike myself. I suppose this is just another thing to add to my list of sins, because I had duped these folks into something, I knew I could never follow through on. Because I actually do have a good singing voice, my mum is a choir singer & I inherited it from her. But when I try to sing it's like there's part of me that's clawing myself back. & my voice comes out timidly, strained, & weak. But one of the things my bandmates never noticed, was the times when they actually did hear me sing, I was totally fucked out of my face on drugs, or totally drunk. It would escape in little windows, where I would start to sing to my potential, but it would have to be singing in a club where the music was deafening, or listening to headphones with my eyes closed, pretending like there was nobody else there. If I was on one of those TV singing contests, I would probably manage one hypersonic squeak before my throat clamped shut, my face turned blue & I keeled over, face first, like an oak tree. I've got a lot of sympathy for anyone who tries, & falls short on one of these shows because of nerves. It's like a self-preservation mechanism, like part of my psyche is convinced that if I start singing then someone's going to stab the fuck out of me.

Wow, I just put two, & two together. My mum was a teacher at my primary school, who led the choir no less. If I had started singing somebody probably would have stabbed the fuck out of me. Part of me thinks that I'm capable of some stunning psychological insights, & self-reflection, but sometimes I just wonder if I'm just so unfathomably obtuse that it defies description. It all seems so obvious now that I lay it out like that. I was always on the defensive in primary school. That's where the fear comes from. But strangely, while that guy was up on-stage playing Metallica to the whole school, I was singing. In front of over a thousand kids, I went up & I sang, a song that nobody wanted to hear admittedly, but I did it. & I got quite a few compliments, & nobody really took the piss, which meant it must have been alright. Only once & never again. I'm weird like that, like I was just trying to make a point to myself. & the only way I could do it was by blocking it out, right up to the second that it happened, I was completely non-committal, maybe I'll do it & maybe I won't. The reason I did it in the end was to help show how amazing a guitarist we had in our midst; he deserved the limelight. Then when it was actually happening it was too much. Never once in your life singing in front of anybody, to suddenly being in front of all these people. It wasn't even scary, because I was in a state of shock, like taking off the blindfold after you've already stepped off the cliff.

& the reason I'm obsessed with the guitar right now is that I'm starting to hear my true voice coming out, a little bit at a time. Not the timid, cowardly, meep, but actually singing. & I'm not claiming to be a great singer, that's not what this is about, it's quite literally about finding your voice. & the guitar is the perfect medium for me to be able to do it. It's like an actor who puts on a great performance, while they are hiding behind a mask of some kind, heavy prosthetics, like Boris Karloff playing the iconic Frankenstein's monster, or Heath Ledger's Joker. Behind the character, behind the paint, the actor can flourish, & the guitar gives me something to focus on, instead of worrying about the act of singing. & over the years writing has been the perfect medium for me to find my voice, I'm not in the least bit blind to the parallel. It seems that finding my true voice is something that's been happening to me a lot recently. & sometimes you have to make that leap of faith, & that's what the 'Poetry of Chaos' was for me, shaky & unsure initially but quickly finding my rhythm. I'm also proud to say that I now know what it's like to sing along as I play the guitar, & the closest thing I can describe it to is like riding a bicycle, or swimming for the first time. A moment of near total disbelief, it's working, fucking hell it's happening, wow! But it quickly becomes natural, & once you've got it, you kind of wonder why it seemed impossible to begin with. Now I'm addicted, & all I want to do is go back, & practice singing, to feel the fear dissipating. & beyond the blistered fingers, the problem is that I only know one song! But to go from nothing to an entire song in one day, what would I have thought when I picked up the guitar yesterday, if I could see how quickly I've progressed?

That was fucking amazing! I just went & played again; it feels like I've been waiting my entire life to express myself like this. I'm not singing too loud, to bug the neighbours or anything, but I'm able to emote more & more each time. I'm only occasionally stifled by the technical complication of what I'm trying to do. Forgetting the next line, or missing a note here & there. But the psychological barriers to my singing are really noticeably falling away, even more so after what I just wrote, that's the beauty of writing, articulation, it really does set you free, & I'm delighted to be able to capture this process for you here. I suppose it's an analogy for anything you want to do in life. To really come to understand yourself, is to be able to breakdown the self-limiting barriers which you perhaps created as a defence mechanism in childhood, which no longer serve you going forward in life. & once you reason out the fears at their root cause, it means that they no longer have a hold over you, & this is an extremely literal demonstration of someone who is setting themselves free, to sing, to express themselves on the page, to be their authentic self without reservation. & you'll just have to take my word for it but my singing is on a completely different level to where it was this morning, & it's not just about practice, it's about letting go! But I'm just getting started here! Not that I have any plans to become a musician or anything, but where will I be in a week or month with this, what will I sound like then? Will it be completely gone, (fingers crossed) the anxiety in my singing voice? Honestly it feels so fucking good! It feels so right! My vocal range is expanding & I'm hitting the individual notes properly, but more than anything it's the emotion that I'm channelling, eyes closed when I hit the chorus, performing with conviction. I can see myself singing in front of people now, which I never envisioned before. & it seems like a silly almost insignificant thing but it matters to me, like a missing piece in the massive jigsaw puzzle that is my true identity. Because in many ways I've been a stranger to myself, & I think everyone is like that, in ways they are not even aware. & maybe I'm more complex than most, or maybe I'm not, I really genuinely don't know. But I think the answer is that everybody has such deep layers of complexity that it's beyond their ability to interpret even a fraction of what's really going on.

So, we tend to cling to over-simplifications, & sometimes that's whole belief systems, religions, political systems, or maybe it's simply individual misperceptions. But we tend to fall into traps of becoming overly rigid in our thinking, as individuals & as groups within society, & it tends to lead to extreme behaviour. Our wishful thinking blinds us to our true underlying motivations, like the narcissistic example of the Stockwell strangler, blaming others for our own undesired traits. Claiming to act in the name of virtue for those who are disenfranchised, using it as a mask for your own darker machinations. Like Dicken's novel, 'A tale of two cities,' or Orwell's 'Animal Farm,' mankind never seems to take full appraisal of the recurring trends within society. & we roll on from barefaced lying tyranny into the inevitable chaos that follows. I firmly believe that it's the responsibility of the individual to come to a deeper understanding of who they are as a person, to manifest their essence in the world. & that is what really creates change at a societal level, & that means the responsibility is on you to save the world! It's up to you to find your voice, to express your soul. & the way to do it is to understand yourself on the deepest of levels. & sometimes it's coming to realise something which is incredibly obvious, which you've simply never stopped to consider. & once you take that leap of faith, perhaps you'll come to find that what once seemed an impossibility becomes completely natural to you. But you can't be afraid to be vulnerable, that's the real challenge!

& as much as my fingers hurt as I'm playing, that is actually a big part of what's spurring me on. It means I can't fuck about; I've got to make it count. So, if I'm really going to sing then I better fucking do it properly, I better do it now! & that's also true of life as well. Sometimes you need to light a fire under your ass, it's the do or die moment that pushes you to excel, to become a better version of yourself. Training is essential, but when it comes time to perform you've got to bring everything you've got! That's life as a whole. Kobe Bryant died just the other day, & LA is in a state of shock. & my heart goes out to all the families affected by that tragedy. I rarely ever watched basketball, but I'd catch a Lakers game, just for him! It doesn't matter who you are, it can happen just like that! Are you bringing it? Are you making the most out of life? Are you showing love? To yourself? To the people who are closest to you in your life? Don't let yourself get dragged into petty bullshit! You've really got to make it fucking count! How you go about doing that is entirely up to you, but I've found some interesting tools which can help make your progress a hell of a lot smoother. Things such as cognitive distortions, mindfulness, stoicism, articulation, the Jungian shadow, chaos theory, the importance of structure, habit forming, objectivity, incremental growth, self-compassion, setting strategies, opening your awareness, seeking alignment, the nature of precision, focus, & creativity. This is how I'm choosing to make the most out of my life, by trying to lessen the unnecessary confusion & suffering in the world through writing, to open myself up, to be vulnerable, & to sing my heart out, without being afraid, or ashamed.

I hope to encourage you to take those first faltering steps, in discovering your own dreams, your own abilities, your own true sense of identity, whatever that is, I want to create a space where you feel free to express yourself, to feel motivated to exceed beyond your wildest expectations, & a place where you feel accepted for the person that you truly are, beyond any psychological defence mechanisms that you may present to yourself, & the world. I ask only that you think, & act with kindness, because that is the true nature of the empowered individual, it is love. It is to bring peace into the world, by first finding peace within yourself. & I so deeply wish peace upon the world that once again my eyes are filled with tears. & I am sitting here in silence, with no songs to induce emotion, it's merely the sentiment which I am expressing here on this page which I feel emanating from the core of my being. It is love, for all those who read these words, & the positive influence you can have on the lives of others, by embracing a depth of self-understanding. Because through true self-analysis you can come to more deeply understand the world, & the behaviours of others. A deeper understanding of self, is a deeper understanding of nature, of the cosmos. A window into an understanding of broader social interaction, & with it a deeper level of compassion, which extends out limitlessly, to the entire of existence, a state of non-duality. What mankind needs are not merely more balanced, joyous, & wise individuals, but a clearer, more accessible, & simpler means of guidance, that's why I'm writing these books, it's a single step in that direction. This is my attempt to make the world a better place, for my having existed in it. It's to try to encourage others to think in the same way, to be truly present, without reservation, & like the tips of my fingers, to be painfully aware, of how precious each moment of your existence, truly is! & why you've got to fucking sing, with everything you've got!

& this is all metaphorical, you don't have to sing, or write, these are just my own personal interests. All you have to do, is express your true nature. But using narcissistic defence mechanisms as an example, that's not always a particularly easy thing to do. But you should go out & find a way to express yourself healthily. I enjoy the traditional creative arts, abstract painting, calligraphy, writing, sketching, singing, guitar, & martial arts. But it doesn't even have to be something like that, it can be what you are already doing, turn your work into a meditation, push yourself to excel. & not everybody is particularly creative, it can be a curse as much as a blessing at times. Maybe your outlet is being productive, simply getting things done. Ideally it should be something which you feel passionate about, & helps to make the world a better place, something that's worth your time. & I've been through slumps in my life where it felt like I wasn't in the least bit creative, & I know it can be infuriating when people tell you to find a passion, especially when you are depressed, you feel like telling them to fuck off, I get it! But you have to take into account that passion is something you have to cultivate. I spent a long time just going through the motions, when it came to writing. & I've written a lot on creative structure, so I'm going to avoid repeating myself here. But I have, as a means of describing the search for the true self, in previous books drawn the parallel with Picasso, who learned to paint traditionally, to a high level, before finding his inner child. Expressing himself in a completely unique fashion. & you'll probably find I do repeat myself, in this book & others, I'm aware of it, I try to avoid it, but I'm also trying to flow naturally, while writing 100's of thousands of words, & sometimes when I go back into the same areas I come to fresh realisations, it's part of the overall process. & this is a cliched piece of advice but don't be afraid of failure, it's a necessary part of the process, if you're not failing then you're not pushing yourself to achieve new things. The truth is you probably already have something which you enjoy, something that interests you, why not explore it a little more deeply, or try a completely new creative hobby? It's all part of coming to realise your potential, getting to know yourself better, seeing yourself from a new perspective.

It's actually the following day now, I picked it up again at the beginning of the last paragraph, & I've just had something of a special moment. This coming Friday I've set a date, I'm going to be going ketogenic, I've done it a couple of times over the last four years, it's quite hardcore, especially when mixed with intermittent fasting. It basically means cutting all the sugar out of your diet, including, bread, pasta, everything. & I got some M&S vouchers for Christmas, so I wanted to get into town, & pick up some goodies before...

Spooky moment. Sorry for the interruption. It's the middle of the night, & I paused momentarily to think of the correct grammar, & my eyes were drawn down to Michael Myers, the serial killer on the cover of the Halloween DVD, on the floor to my right-hand side. While simultaneously the door to the room creaked open ever so slightly, on my left. It was just the wind, or was it? He thinks to himself, getting up to peer speculatively out into the darkness.

Anywaaayyy, I wanted to pick up some pasta & chocolate while I still could. I also wanted to get away from the guitar, before I did myself an injury. They are calling it 'storm Ciara.' The worst in a century, sounds like a bit of a posh bird, doesn't it? She's the one that's creaking my doors, the scary bitch! Worst storm in a century they are calling it! & the coronavirus is making all the headlines at the minute, death toll jumps from around 80 to 800 in a scarily small amount of time. & I'm looking at the spot where I was standing taking notes in the last chapter, you remember 'the heart of the city,' with the pigeons, & all that. & I realise I was standing outside what used to be a lingerie shop, heart of the city indeed? The frilly crotch, more like! & seeing as I was in town to kill some time, I thought I would jump into the cinema, & it was packed. On a Monday afternoon, for a Korean film? I prefer it when it's quiet, which usually isn't an issue with foreign cinema. Unbeknownst to me, 'Parasite' had just won best picture at the Oscars, the first foreign language film to do so. Which goes some way to explaining it, besides it generally being a truly fantastic film. Which left me craving more Korean cinema, so I watched a film called 'Burning,' when I got home, which was very different, but also excellent. Still trying to stop myself from going back to the guitar, but I did eventually.

& I was making myself frustrated, repeatedly failing to get through a couple of verses without missing strings. Concentrating on the notes & forgetting the lyrics, then hitting all the right strings, remembering all the lyrics, & forgetting to change chords. & as I made mistakes, the one thing I wanted most, the attempt to overcome the tentative nature of my singing voice, was frustratingly kept in check. & it wasn't just my fingers, but my shoulder, & also where my foot was propped, everything was getting sorer.

& I was trying to give myself positive self-talk, but the breakthrough wasn't forthcoming. Then I wondered if it would be possible to strum through the chords without having to pick each individual string, just for the meantime while I'm getting used to it, & it worked perfectly. & the second I stopped worrying about the guitar, I stopped worrying about my voice as well.

All day it had been at the back of my mind, tapping my blistered fingers together at the cinema, & smiling to myself. I was thinking about my singing when I was young, & I think one of the real problems, was when my voice dropped. I would have been singing at a higher pitch, but I became too scared to do it as my voice became more difficult to control. & tonight, the poor guitar playing brought out the stress in my voice. & when I simplified everything, it all changed, my voice was leading, & the guitar was flowing along with it. & I felt comfortable singing at a higher pitch, learning to use my guitar like a tuning fork, so confidence in my voice wasn't an issue at all, I was purely in the moment. & as I was now strumming the verse, I rolled naturally into the chorus, which was the easiest, most practiced bit. I could feel the emotion, the vulnerability, my voice soared, & it was a truly beautiful moment! To me, anyway. I could have sounded like a strangled cat for all I know? But now, like a junkie, I'm going back for one last hit before bed. Sweet dreams, my little dumplings!

EMOTIONS

One of the main reasons I write, is to be able to tap into raw emotion. Not necessarily to dig down into old wounds, but to explore a wide range of experiences. I love putting on filmic pieces of music. Right at this moment I'm listening to the Dark Knight soundtrack, & I don't know what the hell I'm going to write about. But I want it to tie in with this astonishing score. I want to feel elated, proud, energised, determined! I want to be able to convey that to the reader, but first & foremost, I want to feel the tingling excitement of creating something new, something which feels honest, & real. I want to match the tone of what I'm hearing, & I want to feel like this soundtrack was created for me in this moment. & you can chalk this up to narcissistic delusion, but when I am in full flow, it feels like I'm saving lives, that my words are carrying over the seemingly impenetrable divide between us, as human beings, & I am truly connecting with the soul of those who read these words. & I imagine them as desperate, lonely, in a dark & dangerous state of mind, like I was as a teenager. & I imagine myself reaching through the complexity, of a seemingly uncaring world, to offer a single ray of hope. A hope that almost extinguished in me, to devastating effect.

I feel most truly alive, when I'm breaking down creative barriers, pushing off into the unknown, with little to no idea of what it is I'm actually trying to do, just as I am in this moment. & it feels like a race against time, a matter of life & death. I need to get heard. I don't even know how in the fuck I'm going to make it happen. But if I'm going to be able to reach out to someone who is on the verge of suicide, or intending to murder indiscriminately, then I have to somehow get these books into people's hands. But I have to first make these books worth reading, they have to jump off the page. You, the reader, have to see & feel the urgency of what is actually going on here. I have to get you to feel it, & see it. I need other people to help me, I need you to help me, I need word of mouth. But I first have to create something worth talking about. I have to create something truly special, funny, heartrending, impactful, unforgettable. Something which is regarded as unmissable. & the only thing I can think to do is be honest, & open, & raw, & as direct as I possibly fucking can! In a way that astonishes people, with fearlessness, & vulnerability. Like my singing voice, I need to throw off every possible inhibition, & express myself at a level which very few people have ever dared to in their lives.

& I am feeling the music right now, I can assure you of that! I'm letting it be my guide, my tuning fork. Hans Zimmer really is, just about, unparalleled. I wish I could directly create an empathic link with you in this moment, to show you the deep exhilaration which I feel. But I'm sure most of you know the music, listening to that is a good way to start. But there's a far greater depth to this. Because it's tied in with what I consider to be the greatest, most important thing which I could possibly do with my life. Writing which breaks through, which changes lives, alters perspectives, pulls people out of self-made traps, re-directs the course of events, creates alternatives which they themselves could not have previously envisioned. & like the Picasso image, finding his creativity, painting with his inner child, another image I've used repeatedly is that of a fly buzzing against a window. From the years of working on suicide lines I saw this same problem over, & over, & over, & over again. To get caught in a loop, psychologically, I've been like that myself, especially being on the autistic spectrum. & my books, in particular 'The Optimal Path,' is my way of opening a window, explaining things in the simplest of terms, to gently usher people through, to set them free, from the traps they've created for themselves. & I've said this repeatedly as well, these books are aimed at the confused, & fucked up kid that I used to be. The one under the blade in that graveyard, the one with the death-wish in his eyes.

I'm fighting to save people's souls, I genuinely am. & the more I write, the more deeply convinced I am of that fact. & as time slips past the more desperate that struggle feels. So, that's why the music pulses through me, because I need it. I need the energy; I need the inspiration. I need it to put me in the appropriate mindset, & there is no other piece of music that I would turn to for this. Because it feels like hope, in a state of true desperation, the ability to respond through a depth of self-belief, & it carries an unceasing urgency. It's not about becoming a hero; it's about doing what needs to be done. & I need to somehow get you to feel this fucking music, to sense that ticking clock. In my mind this all ties in with social media, that's part of why I went into so much depth on it. Because I envision the number of spree killings is going to keep steadily rising. As people get more isolated, emotionally detached, anxious, frustrated. I'm thinking about the lives of families affected by real world tragedies. Because I came so fucking close myself, without having somebody directly reaching out to me, in the way that I am trying with these books. Everything has become focused on this endeavour, & I don't know how the fuck I'm going to lighten the tone, & what the fuck else I'm going to be able to talk about for the rest of this book. But it's always just one sentence, one chapter at a time. The blade is still under the throat, & the countdown is still ticking down, 10, 9, 8, those families don't know what's headed in their direction, 7, 6, 5, & it's all completely fucking avoidable, 4, 3, 2, I'm the voice in the darkness, calling out at the last second, creating that one window of opportunity, for things to turn out differently, that's all I'm doing, & if you are the one with the blade or gun in your hand, I'm giving you an out.

Because it doesn't have to end in tragedy, & bloodshed, it really fucking doesn't. Because I know what it's like to be angry at existence, & to want to see the world burn, I so fucking genuinely do! But it is simply a matter of perspective, a trick of the light, it can all completely change. Everything you are wrapped up in, all of the obsessions which you can't see past, even your own self-perception, all of it can change! & chances are, it probably would change, naturally, over time. & when you are the fly that's buzzing endlessly up against the window it can be impossible to see that, because you lack objectivity, well, guess what motherfucker? That's where I come in! I am the voice of objectivity! The voice of reason, love, & compassion! Because though you might feel like nobody in the world cares about you, I am sitting at this keyboard fucking screaming it in your face! This isn't just about those which you could hurt by your actions, this is about you, the angry, misunderstood, alienated person, who feels like life isn't fair, can't ever be fair, & wants nothing more than to manifest their frustrations in absolute carnage. There're certain factors you have to take into account. Usually when we reach breaking point, it's when a number of problems come together at once, it's like a perfect storm. Your whole life is thrown into chaos, by a series of events which cause you to feel completely overwhelmed by complexity. & these moments invariably pass, like the crest of a wave, an inevitable rise & fall. Perhaps there's an underlying issue which you are refusing to deal with which is fuelling all these negative emotions. A lot of our resentment comes when others don't live up to our expectations. So, imagine you are living with a false self, any insult or injury to that is like an assault on the god which you worship, an almost unthinkable act. But in my case, I'd long since lost touch with reality when my breaking point came. & in some ways it was a necessary process, that's the craziest fucking part.

Sometimes a seeming breakdown, can actually be a life changing breakthrough of sorts. A chance to let go of the misperceptions which have built up over time. An opportunity to choose a new direction in life, to change your social setting. I wouldn't be sitting here writing if it wasn't for that very process.

After going into hospital, I started creative writing as therapy, laid on by my psychiatrist & the NHS. We wouldn't be here if I wasn't a nutter to begin with. But over time there was a complete, & radical transformation. Instead of hating the entire of existence, I feel the polar opposite. Instead of wanting to kill indiscriminately, I want nothing more than to help save lives! & my reward for that endeavour at this exact moment in time is to feel the vibration of this incredibly intense music, right down in the core of my being. It's to feel an urgent passion, a clear sense of purpose. & with that sense of purpose, with a clear & certain aim, everything else has, or is in the process of, falling into alignment with it! It's the reason for the tears as I sit & write, as I look out the window on my way to work. Tears of joy, on the way to the dentist? Who lives like that? This is the very nature, of the optimal path!

Over the years I have been writing, not only to fuel, & capture my radical transformation, but to encourage others to believe in their own ability to change, & to layout in simple terms, how I personally go about balancing my perspective. & that's what it comes down to, walking the line, that is the nature of peace, sustaining a certain frequency of being. & it is natural, that's the overlooked simplicity of it all. It's how you would be, if you weren't continuously chasing after hollow aspirations, head fucked by chemicals, & the psycho-social manipulation of mass consumerism, etc, etc, etc. & like me finding my singing voice, it's all a matter of learning to let go! Letting go of emotional trauma, extremist brainwashing, the historical baggage of dead people, aspirational lifestyles, existential angst, fear of the other, the illusion of the false-self, the underlying belief that there is something inherently wrong with you, an unspoken sense of shame, misperceptions carried from childhood, & on, & on, & on. Fuck all that bullshit!!! You are not irrelevant, your actions are not irrelevant, the absolute opposite is true. You are important, you are incredibly important, what you choose to do can have massive effects, completely beyond your comprehension. So, stop fucking about!

Get your shit together! Do something which you can be proud of! & I'm not just writing to a younger version of myself, I'm writing to everyone, I'm writing to mankind, to generations not yet born. I'm just another human being, amongst trillions of human beings, but I've found love, & peace, & joy, everything which the soul desperately craves. In this moment I have it all at my fingertips, & I wish nothing but peace, & joy upon you all. I'm not some perfect, infallible entity, this is far from unattainable, I'm not different to the average person. The only difference is a very particular point of focus, my entire existence has been about this. Even when I was tearing myself apart psychologically, everything was about achieving this state, finding this elusive truth. & you're going to fucking hate me for this, but it comes right back to the world's oldest cliché. The answer is already inside you. There's nothing more that need be attained, nothing you have to figure out, that's the infuriating truth. The answer to the meaning of life, existence, the cosmos, is being itself! Consciousness. To become completely aware of it, is to attain a state of non-duality, to be at one with the universe, in harmony. For me this is the nature of what people call god, & without having any specific connection to any particular faith, this is something I feel a strong & literal connection to, especially in moments such as this, when I'm flowing, being creative, & open. This is my place of worship, behind the keyboard. It is the practice of being present, constantly. Meditation is really just the start. It is to attain a deeper level of awareness through persistent attention, & it takes time, & dedication.

It is now the following day, I'm just back from work, & I'm probably more hyped right now than I was last night. Because I was listening to the Dark Knight Trilogy on the way home, staring up at Glasgow's gothic architecture from the window of the bus. Building myself up for this moment, just another overlooked commuter, but inside I felt charged, with a dramatic intensity. I call it 'earning the music,' doing something of such value & importance that the right kind of music fills you with overwhelming emotion, literally brings tears to your eyes. It's not just when I sit to write, sometimes it's when I least expect it, listening to music, looking out a window, the tears suddenly streaming down my cheeks. It's the most wonderful sensation, it's to feel that you are engaged in something which is truly significant. It's the opposite of a self-seeking obsession, to become rich, drive a fancy car, all that kind of stuff. This is about helping change the quality of people's lives, maybe not even saving them, maybe just easing the self-hatred which so many people are consumed by. To be felt, to be understood, that's what I want to do for people. To reach out to those who feel broken inside, to those who are going through a deep existential crisis, to those who are stuck in self-defeating downward spirals, ostracised, invisible. Those who feel like life isn't fair, & there's no way out of their current situation, without resorting to violence, against others, & against themselves. This is for all the people who are trapped in a state of desperation, frantically looking for a way out.

I don't know what you've been through, or what you have to endure on a daily basis? All I can do is talk from personal experience, but sometimes when one thing after another goes wrong, & your life seems irreparably fucked, sometimes the only option is hospitalisation. Just to get you out of the immediate storm. We all need help, we all need to talk, open up, we all need to feel heard sometimes. & I've sat with counsellors & psychiatrists where I might as well have been talking to a brick wall, but it gave me an opportunity to hear myself. Trying to work out what's going on in your psyche is like trying to solve an insanely complex mathematical equation, but when you are able to lay things out, by talking, by writing, it helps you join the dots. & if you have somebody who's wise to talk to, then they will help point out the simple little things which you might have overlooked. So, I'm talking about every subject I can think of, rumination, persistence, depression, anxiety, narcissism, trauma, dieting, inter-personal relationships, social infrastructure, social media, self-awareness, catastrophising, etc, etc, in the hope that some of it resonates with you. I'm trying to lay out everything a person could possibly need to know in order to make themselves psychologically functional, because we can all be a little delusional in our own way, at some point we've probably fallen into all of these traps. But I work with violent schizophrenics, & sometimes the only way to avert a crisis, is to remove them from the situation, to leave the premises, find someplace quiet, an opportunity to chill out, & let the overwhelming sensations pass. That's what I mean, when I'm talking about hospitalisation, sometimes acting crazy is almost rational, because it's the situation which is out of control. & what you have to do is extricate yourself from it, get out of abusive relationships, get away for a while, maybe just take a walk, to stop you from acting out of aggressive impulse. & the first thing I would advise you to do is learn how to take a deep breath, not a whole meditation, just a single solitary breath. To slow down, refocus, a single moment which shuts out the chaos, which allows you to centre yourself, stop, let go, & start again. The more meditation practice you do, the more effective this practice is. Try closing your eyes, emptying your mind, gently fill your lungs, let your shoulders relax. Hold it for a moment, & then gently exhale. Think of it like a moment of rebirth, turning off & restarting a computer, just give yourself that little moment to reset, to find a little shred of rationality before you actively make the situation worse.

But that same process of rebirth can be mirrored in a major structural collapse, when your entire life seemingly falls apart. & that's what hospital was for me, everything changed, I had to let go of so much. There was a very clear before & after, but it was exactly what I needed at that time. It wasn't that I was suddenly fixed, but I left my problems outside. Then it was a long slow process of rebuilding, going through college, university, volunteering, building up to the life that I have now. But it's quite common for creative people to go through this kind of process, to put so much psychological & emotional pressure on themselves that they disintegrate, & have to start from nothing. I say it's natural, because this is the very nature of chaos & order, it's the same on an individual level, as it is on a societal level. Excessive order creates tyranny, which leads to the chaos of revolt, & out of the chaos a new structure emerges. It's the Yin Yang symbol, out of light comes darkness, & out of darkness comes light, it's a cycle which is replicated by the ventricles of your beating heart. Order is as essential to your heart as chaos is to the electrical patterns of the brain, something I go into more depth on in the 'Optimal Path' series.

But it all seems to fit into patterns, like the structure of narrative storytelling, it's the darkest hour which the protagonist goes through, at the end of the second act. & there's something hardwired in the human psyche, throughout the course of history, to recognise story structure, regardless of race, or nationality. It is the story of the hero. There seems to me a very clear connection between the way a river flows, a tap drips, trees grow, the heart beats, society functions, your mind works. It's all interconnected, it's the very nature of existence itself, the same laws of gravitational attraction, wave functions, spiralling loops, I don't necessarily have the vocabulary to explain it all, but I feel it. The intellect is not the path to contentment, & an obsessive imbalance can lead to an existential crisis. The most important thing I ever did, was let go of the need to dissect existence, & open my awareness. Now, I daily recognise little connections, all around me, purely by attentive observation. & on a personal level what every human being truly desires, though they don't fully comprehend it, or act accordingly, is balance. It's what the Christian's call the 'Narrow Gate,' & Buddhists call the 'Middle Way.' It requires a life dedicated to this pursuit, training yourself to live in harmony with the universe. I presume most religions have their own version of this teaching. But I am less interested in religious texts than I am in pragmatic, lived experience. It's about opening your awareness, truly feeling what is going on, again this incredibly dramatic music, which is still playing in the background, comes to the forefront of my attention! Terminology is a difficult thing, being 'at one' with something, it's not language which we commonly use, except in a grandiose, & abstract sense. But feeling it! You get what I mean by that? Like the best concert you've ever been to, or eating something delicious when you've been hungry for hours. Really savouring something so much, that it makes you feel more alive. We all have moments of experience like that, sometimes terrifying, sometimes beautiful, usually rare, but I'm talking about having wilful access to that, to be able to have astonishingly deep experiences, every single day! & more than that, to feel yourself part of a greater truth, a deep connection to existence itself. With absolutely no fear of death, & an overwhelming love, & exuberant energy which you can put into whatever activity you desire. & that is why you need to find a passion, something to master, it's your pathway to transcendent experience. But if you understand a depth of mastery, at a level where you can use dramatic abstraction, you can use the insights you gain from that process to analyse & observe processes across multiple fields. But the process of mastery isn't something which you can attain from reading a book, it takes time & effort. But not every elite tennis player, or footballer, is a zen master. But the arts which you choose to master can be a window into the transcendental, if you learn how to lose yourself in them. It's not uncommon for me to burn through more than seven hours at a time, when I'm writing.

But for me the real breakthroughs come with moments of deep realisation. Everything suddenly seems to fall into place, & I'm then permanently altered by these life changing events. I've had around four or five, super-massive realisations that I can think of, off the top of my head. Moments which left me feeling, not just psychologically, but physically altered. If there was one thing which really did make me different to other people then it would probably be that, & this is already ground that I've covered in 'The Playmaker.' But I don't necessarily mean having to go this deep, dedicating your entire life, that's the role of the sage, not everybody is wired up the same. I'm not trying to sell you on the full package, there might be some very specific people out there for whom these books are exactly what they've been looking for, but I'm talking to the whole world here. There are some very small, & simple steps which you can take, which will most likely transform your entire life, for the better. If you refuse to put ten minutes aside for meditation, then look up 'one breath meditation' online, give that a try. Find something which grounds you in the present moment, by far the best thing I've ever found is to look at nature. Just for a minute, or however long you like, put everything else aside, & just observe. The leaves in the trees, the flight of birds, a passing cloud, allow yourself to tune in to that regularly, & when your mind wanders don't get upset, just bring yourself back into the moment. & make a habit of observing yourself, pay attention to what you say & do, try to be self-aware without being judgemental. & try to live with compassion, not just for others, but also yourself. This is a major part of the 'Optimal Path,' but kindness does not mean indulgence, it means nurture, making small decisions to encourage self-discipline. & this starts with habit forming, pick something, & it can be as easy as you like, the decision to spend three minutes stretching in the morning, & stick to it. Without question, without reticence, like a robot, every morning, 3 minutes (this is just an example.) Then over time you can build upon that routine, at a speed that's comfortable to you, until it becomes like second nature. Over time with incremental growth, one step at a time, you can achieve phenomenal results.

Can you imagine a world where everybody was actively self-aware, living more fully in the moment, deliberately compassionate to others, building self-nurturing lifestyles, & taking a deep meditative breath before acting out of anger, & frustration? It sounds so incredibly simple, but simplicity can be the hardest thing to master. The problem comes with self-sabotage, a lack of persistence. & my routines are constantly knocked out of synch by one lifestyle change or another. But you just have to put your frustrations aside, & simply go back to what you were doing, whether it's dieting, addiction, or whatever. Knowing that failure is part of the process, is a massive step toward accomplishing the goals you set for yourself in life. If you become a tyrant to yourself then you will hit a point of fatigue, when that happens the structure collapses, & chaos ensues. The nature of the middle path, is one of gentle compassion, patience, & strength through persistence. As far as I'm concerned, you don't have to adhere to any particular religious faith to see the wisdom in a balanced perspective, all you need to do is look at is the genocidal insanity of extremist ideologies in the 20th century, on both sides of the political spectrum. But the balance of chaos & order requires a continual process of navigation, that's why you need to talk, to understand yourself more deeply, to stop you from tearing yourself apart. Which brings us full circle, back to what I was talking about when we started this chapter, I write so that I can express emotion. I have used it to dig deep into my childhood, & address the misperceptions which caused me to bottle up my emotions, but I also write to play with emotion. I love to freak myself out with scary stories, making myself laugh, I love just letting my imagination flow. & that's the nature of someone who is in a state of alignment, it brings a certain playful eccentricity. & what I want more than anything else, is for us to simply have fun!

RESILIENCE

You know how people say, 'bad luck comes in threes.' Well, this is more like an unceasing wave. & it's not like anybody close to me is dying (fingers crossed.) But instead, it's an endless series of silly little niggly things, all going wrong, one after another. & the bigger stuff I don't even want to get into, because it would take too long to explain. I go to put on my jacket, the zip rips off. I go downstairs, the door to the close has been kicked in. I end up walking around an industrial estate in the pouring rain, looking for a post office to pick up a package, when a truck hits a puddle, & douses me. I get to the post office, & the package has already been returned to sender. A couple of months out of last year I would have been financially better off unemployed, & I was depending on a decent amount of accrued holiday pay, & that's fallen through. These are just examples of an overall trend, & I'm left wondering what's next? But as the bus I'm waiting on, goes the wrong way through a roundabout & bypasses me entirely, leaving me standing in the rain, I have a big smile on my face, because fuck it! It's not that life is never going to be perfect, it's that it's always perpetually going to be fucked! If you allow your disposition to be determined by external circumstances then you are going to be an incredibly miserable person, living a very unpleasant existence. Because there will always be a stone in your shoe, something not right, something which needs fixing, some irksome, inconvenient, bastardly little thing, just waiting to ruin your day.

People who suffer from autism often find very small things incredibly troubling. In extreme cases a break in routine, or things out of place can lead to full blown panic attacks. Personally, I've always struggled with financial things, filling out forms, admin, that kind of stuff. & on some level I attribute it to autism. I'm not comfortable until things have been taken care of, & I've learned to try & sort everything as quickly as possible, & I rely on lists to let me know what I need to attend to, & when. During the period that my life fell apart, I went into total denial, when a bill came through, I remember stuffing them behind a chest of drawers. When you're doing crazy shit like that then you really are not coping. I just didn't want to think about it, I wanted the whole world to fuck off! Just let me sink into a bottle of cider, pop some pills, & get it all to fuck. A couple of days ago my smile had faded, & I was starting to wonder if I was being punished on some level for having sounded so upbeat in the last chapter. Joyful, are you? We'll see about that! I'm as superstitious as an old sea captain, & I was wondering if I'd jinxed myself?

But the first thing you need when you're feeling low is self-awareness. I realised instantly that I was suffering from a cognitive distortion, I was filtering out all the negative things, & ignoring the positive. Then I made a list of positive things in my life to be thankful for, top of that list is always my loved ones. But when I stopped to appraise my overall situation, I was able to rebalance my perspective.

Because I had just started intermittent fasting, & I was ketogenic, there were sugar cravings, & a hunger I hadn't felt in quite some time. & those physical sensations had attached to my financial problems, & I was starting to obsess about how unfair it all seemed. I'll sometimes find that I'm worried about something, but I've actually got a dull headache, or something to that effect, that I haven't acknowledged. Once you realise that these are actually misinterpreted signals, then it removes some of the power that they hold over you. My way of simplifying the way that I work internally is to think of everything as energy.

For example, perhaps you experienced trauma when you were a child, that energy gets trapped, it creates an emotional blockage, which leads to other problems, denial, self-comforting, etc. Like flowing water, repetition creates deep pathways. Over time that energy can fester, it can turn into rage, & can manifest in destructive forms. Sometimes, for example, a blockage can come from the need to understand the nature of being, which leads to an existential crisis, which is what caused my downward spiral. The healthy thing to do is to release the pent-up energy which causes discomfort in your life. This allows you to grow as an individual, & live a contented life. There is an appropriate time to deal with the innumerable problems which life throws at you, but it's quite common to be lost in thought, surrounding your overall situation. Letting go of that is what allows you to be more fully present, more fully alive. Ask yourself, why? What is upsetting you? The answer might be something you really don't expect, a repressed emotion, which has been left unaddressed for many years. What you need to develop is a curiosity, like a detective trying to unriddle a mystery, what is really going on? It may be that you need professional help, but there's a great quantity of free self-help tools online, my advice though is to start with cognitive distortions.

But psychology is only one part of the equation. If your thoughts are out of balance then they will only serve to distract you. So, it's not something to be overlooked, but it is not the source of peace & contentment, that is to be found within you. The best example is that of children at play, that exuberant energy is at the heart of the human spirit. We want nothing more than to love, & to be loved, to be seen, heard, appreciated. We want to have fun, & be expressive. We want to be understood at the deepest of levels, & we struggle. We struggle to find the right words, to meet the right people, & to first understand ourselves. & we get frustrated, & angry, & bitter, & resentful. & all that beautiful energy gets warped & corrupted, till we've got kids running around schools with semi-automatic weaponry. &

life is complicated. We have animalistic drives, our need for security becomes greed, the ego falls in love with itself, everybody has impulses, sudden, inexplicable, anti-social, violent, half-repressed, maladaptive, misinterpreted, urges. Sexual desires, peer pressure, jealousy, expectations, conformity. The rules of acceptability are a fluid construct, & media formats keep changing. Just a couple of generations ago, your identity was laid out for you, people just did what was expected of them, these were issues that for the most part they never even considered. But if you look past all the confusion, if you can silence the chattering mind, & if you approach it from a balanced perspective, you will find there is joy in you, an energy which emanates from your core. Life can be excessively cruel, & hardships can completely overwhelm you, but that is the very nature of what you are, you are a loving creature. & that energy can be warped & corrupted to the most twisted genocidal extreme, the most horrific, horrendous extremes. But that is the nature of consciousness, it is love, it is light, it is joyous, & caring, everything that is good in the world. & I just want to have fun, because I want to bathe in that energy, & to show you what it's like, to be in love with existence.

Today I watched a video of a philosopher, who was aged 97, & had lectured for 40 years. He was thinking about death, asking himself, 'what is the point of it all?' He always felt like he was missing something, 'in this argument,' & in the end it was a 'foolish question, without any good answer.' At one point he was talking about looking at the trees in his garden, for the first time it seemed like a transcendent experience. From my perspective, that was the answer. It is not a thing to be argued, put your philosophy aside, the answer is something to be felt, to be lived. It is consciousness experiencing itself. It is a depth of awareness which brings transcendent experience, & for all his years of philosophy, he could not see the answer that was right in front of him, the whole time. This is not a game of words, & opinions. Regardless of who you are, the culture into which you were born, or the beliefs which were instilled in you, nothing is as certain as the falling rain, the touch of air upon your skin. There is a war of ideas raging in the minds of people all over the world, but if they were to embrace true stillness, they would be confronted by a single undeniable truth, reality itself. You may not be satisfied by this answer, it may seem overly simplistic, but it is the path to peace, joy, & contentment. Be in the moment, still your mind, open your awareness, this is all you need to do. Once you've truly mastered that, then everything else follows on from it. Judgement no longer clouded by ego, not viewing the world from the perspective of the false-self, engaging with others at a deeper level, your actions fuelled by altruistic intentions. In touch with a more fulfilling experience of life, you will allow yourself to open up, & find strength through vulnerability. In touch with your essence, at a deeper than animalistic level, your natural spirit shining through. Laughing, playing, creative, passionate, inquisitive. You will appreciate life & will start thinking to the future, & you will start to act accordingly, putting aside everything that does not serve you, addictions, obsessions, you will start to embrace self-nurture without reticence, because you care about your own life, & the quality of it. You will start to understand what I mean by the importance of finding balance, you will experience the benefits of it in your own life, & appreciate the freedom that it brings. It is not a foolish question, but to one who practices a depth of awareness, the answer is self-explanatory.

After an insipid & ill-advised dinner of raw vegetables, other than one black coffee for breakfast, all I've had is water over the last 16 hours. & there's a kid on the bus who is really stretching his lungs, I don't know what the issue is but he sounds like someone's trying to take his foot off with a rusty saw. On the way out this morning there was a note in the stairwell, saying the package is now at another location, ready for pickup. Wrong name on the slip, I assume there's been a fuck up, & I might not be able to collect it. While on the way to work my boss phones to confirm that I won't be getting paid next month, the kid is still screaming. I don't actually want this package, but apparently my internet is about to get switched off, & I need to replace the hub. What I want is to just be left alone! My hunger is attaching to the scream, but I'm aware of it, my mind is ruminating on my financial issues. I catch myself doing it, & I start to smile.

It is in these moments when we realise that we're trapped in rumination that we tend to chastise ourselves; this is a mistake. In this moment you have become self-aware, it is a good thing. The key to a resilient attitude is to be patient, especially with yourself. Life is full of setbacks, but the real discomfort comes from the way we react. We tear at ourselves in frustration, sometimes even when a situation is out-with our control. We can be surrounded by beautiful scenery, but oblivious to it because we are fretting over things we can't change in that moment. You may have peace & joy inside you, but they still need to be cultivated, especially with all the distractions which come with modern life. We cause ourselves consternation by ruminating on problems, & you can address this in a number of ways. You can dig down to the root of the issue, if it's some deep held misconception. You can raise your level of awareness, as I chose to on the bus, letting go of thoughts entirely, & focusing on the scenery. You don't need scenery for this, you can concentrate on your breath, the most common of meditations. & you can also fill your life with other things, for me it's writing. Instead of ruminating on my problems, & feeling sorry for myself, I've been spending the last couple of days thinking about how I could best present them to you, in a way which might be helpful. It's also helped me remain extremely self-aware, because I'm making a mental note of events, & my reactions. But having a project that requires mental stimulation, which gives the mind something positive to work on, will help save you from over-analysing every insignificant problem that arises. Being focused on writing over the last couple of days has also meant that I've remained completely objective. The events that I've captured are so insignificant as to be laughable, these are the small issues which come & go, which are completely forgotten about in a couple of months, but there was a time not so long ago that I would have spent most of my time worrying, fretting, catastrophising. What if my internet gets switched off, what if I can't pay the bills, what if, x, y, z. & somewhere along the line my frustration would need a target, & today it would have been the person who left the note in the middle of the stairwell, instead of putting it through the appropriate letter-box, very unprofessional, but I would be blaming them for the van that doused me the previous day, I'd be blaming them for the hunger, the screaming kid on the bus. I'd be cursing them on some level, unable to let go of it, till everything fell into the background. 'Who fucking does that? Leaves it right in the middle of the close? How inconsiderate can you get? Too lazy to walk up a flight of stairs, you need reporting! UPS, how do you pronounce that? Is it OOPS? Motherfucking son of a...' & the world is filled with people all walking around, looking for some way to vent their frustration, because the setbacks never cease, the stress, the aggro, the bullshit, it never stops! Especially when you are carrying it all inside you, letting it fester into something extremely ugly, a neurosis, a stroke, a tumour.

& staring up at the near luminous green mould on the window ledges on the corner of West Regent Street, on my way home, I still have that same great big smile on my face, because I honestly couldn't care less. I have a good life, & I know it (fingers crossed!) I have so much to be thankful for, & as long as I can keep my perspective balanced, these things have no power over me. Because it would be so easy to become fixated on these everyday complaints, & people do, they really, really do. Until they become completely overwhelmed, & I have all the sympathy in the world, because I've been there myself. I'm not making light of this issue because it can seem like the end of the world when you can't see past it. There can be any number of things which people just can't compute, the audacity of others, casual neglect, or mistreatment, at home or in the work place. They may seem like nothing to the perpetrator, but can create a psychological block for others which can be quite devastating. & when your head gets stuck in that loop, replaying it over, & over, you are driving yourself crazy. You need someone to snap you out of it, & here's me slapping you upside the head, & telling you that you can do it for yourself. You can pull yourself out of most loops, through self-awareness, through objectivity, by understanding your defence mechanisms, & cognitive distortions. But honestly, the best tip is when you realise you are ruminating on a problem, don't beat yourself up about it, take a big cleansing breath, put your thoughts aside, & concentrate on your senses. Literally feel yourself present in this moment, your breath, the air against your skin. Take the time to put things into perspective, find the things you are grateful for, be aware of the patterns that you fall into, the same thoughts repeating themselves. When you do this, the thoughts themselves remind you that you are in a distracted state. Do not be angry when you find yourself ruminating, because it is in this moment that you are becoming self-aware. & like anything else, the more you practice, the easier it becomes.

One of the major issues, which obviously relates back to narcissism, is the ego. If you have an inflated ego, you will be prone to greed, envy, pride, every sin in the book basically. & I don't want you to think I'm being moralistic here, or finger wagging, but self-obsession is extra baggage. It makes you more reactionary, more easily butthurt. & you will react by self-medicating, seeking attention, most likely from the wrong kind of people, looking for any kind of way to numb the pain. This is obviously somebody talking from experience here, so once again, I am really not passing judgement! But if you look at the electrical patterns of a person's brain after just a few months of meditation, you will see that the area considered the ego-centre, calms right down. That's the nature of what I'm talking about, if you want to change your life, let go of the anxiety, the stress, & pressure, you have to put in the effort to start meditating regularly. & for all the fasting, mindfulness, & meditation in my daily life, I'm not a monk! I take only what I find to have practical applications from the thought systems I have studied. I am not trying to convert you to any particular school of philosophy, or religion. I'm only laying out the benefits which I have found from practices such as present moment awareness, balancing my lifestyle, finding a sense of purpose. & perhaps the greatest advancement which I've made in my quality of life, comes from the psychological resilience which I'm describing to you in this chapter. Because though these are seemingly insignificant events, they tend to make up a large part of everyday life, & it is the way you relate to things on a regular basis that has the most profound effect on your experience of life. The way in which you interpret small problems can have an astronomical impact on your emotional state, your overall perspective as a human being. & when you break it down to such a degree, you can start to see that it becomes a matter of identity, it is a major part of who you are! Are you a worrier? Are you constantly distracted, rarely giving of your time & attention to others? Do you appreciate the little things in life? How alive do you really feel? How reliant are you on sugar, alcohol, tobacco, social media, approval, narcotics, drama, or whatever your fix is? Are you emotionally self-reliant? Are you gentle with yourself & others? Are you patient, resilient, confident, resourceful? & are you truly at peace?

But I suppose the question you ought to be asking yourself, is 'why should I take advice off of somebody who is flat broke?' Well, I can't really argue with that one. I do have some financial advice though, don't try & become a writer, & forget about film school. The truth is I could go out & earn more money if I was so inclined, but I've never really been that fussed about it, as long as I've got enough to get by. & I'm not saying you should stop drinking, stop spending money, stop smoking, or whatever you are into (you probably should stop smoking actually.) It's your level of dependency which is the issue, because it's the coping mechanisms that grind you down over time. & I'm always conscious about appearing high & mighty, telling other people what they should do, but it's really not about that! Go binge, have an orgy, knock yourself out, it's none of my business. All I'm trying to do, is wake people up to their own avoidance, to help break them out of self-destructive patterns. Because that's what I've had to do for myself, & life honestly gets better without the crutch of addiction. I took a lot of drugs, & I drank to ridiculous excess, but ultimately it was all just a distraction, & I'm no longer prepared to waste my life like that. Now I'm focusing my energy into being creative, strengthening my focus, & appreciating every moment of my existence, to the best of my abilities. & I'm certainly not going to waste my life ruminating on pointless shit, because if worrying is part of your general disposition, then there will always be something new for you to worry about!

Despite living in a privileged society, born into a loving home, with stable parents, when my whole world started to fall apart, I felt completely alone. The vast percentage of my problems were completely avoidable, because I was at war with myself. Our society isn't designed to offer guidance with any of the emotional problems which I went through. This fundamental problem is a large part of the mental health epidemic. This is why I've written in excess of 200,000 words in the last eight months, it is to prevent the unnecessary suffering of people all over the world. I don't want people to have to go through what I did, to feel alone, & angry at existence. I want to help people before they reach their own personal crisis point, & that is my motivation. That is the fuel that drives my actions. It is part of the reason that I'm not drunk right now, that I'm taking care of my diet, getting my routines in order. I would rather have the time to write, than put money in my own pocket. Having a deep sense of purpose, is what makes you truly resilient! So, you have to find what matters most to you, on the deepest of levels. You have to learn to care, about something more than yourself. My dreams are very big! I want to help the world, & to do that you have to dedicate your entire life to such a cause, & that is what I am doing. In the face of which, these everyday little inconveniences are absolutely nothing! Having a clear & direct purpose changes your entire perspective on life, it can make you stronger than you ever believed possible, & with real persistence you can achieve miracles!

Resilience is something which can either be built up or broken down over time, you can end up getting worn down. The question is, how are you handling your resources? Are you allowing rumination to get the better of you? Are you constantly catastrophising, anxious, & depressed? Are you always fighting a hangover, or a come down? Are you eating, & sleeping properly? Are you facing up to your problems, or hiding from them? Find something about which you care, & fight for it! Choose to be a stronger person, one tiny little decision at a time!

SMOTHERING

Heather did just about everything for her mother. It wasn't in the least bit necessary, but that's how she'd been raised. Moira was far from an invalid, & yet Heather helped her dress, cooked for her, chauffeured her, & ran her baths, without a word of complaint. Because she was a good girl, as her mother would say, or as a psychologist might phrase it, because of 'parasitic co-dependency issues.' They both dressed alike, at her mother's insistence. 'They were just like twins;' her mother would often say. & yet, it was Heather who was made to stand in attendance, like a hand maiden, helping her put on her pearls, brushing her mother's hair. & Heather was always second into the bath, after Moira was finished with the bathwater. Her father had killed himself just a week prior, & it was Heather who had found the body, hanging in the study. She'd seen it coming, over time he'd become more insulated, withdrawn. But Moira never stopped. Sniping at him, whinging like a rusted gate. Casting aspersions on everything he ever did, or ever was, a failed wretch. Now a saint, a lost & dearly departed saint, who could do no wrong, whose example Heather would do well to live up to! Whatever had possessed the poor man, to take his own life? Who was the villain, the culprit? The accountancy firm which had worked his fingers to the bone? That horse's ass of a GP? The finger of blame eternally pointing elsewhere. But Heather wasn't blind to it, she said nothing, she did nothing, except for what she was told. & her mother had become all the more demanding since her father's death, an event which she had yet to even begin to process. Heather was already clinically obese, & her eating habits were bordering on hyperphagia, so her weight had been steadily rising, which was causing further distress.

'Are you not listening to me girl? I said we're going to lose the house, we're virtually penniless. We're going to be homeless; don't you understand?' Said Moira, her voice so posh that it quavered slightly around the vowels.

Heather was driving the car. Moira was sitting in the passenger seat, pulled out a cigarette, & lit it.

'If you have to smoke mum, can you at least open a window?'

Moira turned & looked at her like she might slap her in the face if she wasn't driving the car. But Heather kept her eyes on the road. She found it helped if she didn't look at her mother's face, when she was trying to make herself heard. It was best to avoid that withering stare. She would always remember her father in the last years of his life, perpetually staring at his own feet. Grudgingly Moira rolled down the window, but continued to blow smoke directly in Heather's face.

'Homeless, does that not even register with you?'

'Well mum, I may have a solution.'

'What on earth are you talking about?'

'Take a look in the glove compartment.'

Moira opened it, & pulled out a small, black, satin box.

'What's this?'

'It's an engagement ring.'

Moira opened the box & inspected the petite diamond ring inside.

'Who's it from?'

'Johnathan, obviously.'

'That oik from the fish market?'

'He doesn't work at a fish market.'

'He certainly smells like he does.'

'He's in I.T. He works with computers.'

Moira took the ring out of the box & turned it from side to side, to inspect it.

'Did he find this in a packet of cornflakes?' Heather let this derisive comment pass.

Moira put the ring back in the box & snapped it shut.

'Well, you'll just have to give it back.'

'I most certainly will not!'

Heather had reacted without thought, never in her life had she been as forthright with her mother, spoken to her in such an authoritative tone. But she did love John, & she would be married, she wouldn't let anything stop that, not even mother. Then for a fleeting instant she was proud of herself, for finding her voice, for speaking out at last. But this moment of triumph was short lived, as Moira without saying a word, threw the ring out the window.

A part of Heather was permanently lost in that act. John had laid out a trail of rose petals for her to follow, in an overblown romantic gesture, but she didn't think it too much. Surrounded by candles he had dropped to one knee, expressing his undying love, asking for her hand in marriage. In that moment she was made to feel like the princess she'd always felt herself to be. Locked away in a tower, her dragon of a mother chasing off suitors. She didn't feel attractive, too self-conscious about her weight. But John was overweight too, & saw her differently, made her see herself differently. & she had dared to dream, about a new life, one that was filled with possibilities. & she knew her mother would object, but she'd make her see. If only she understood their love, she would understand.

The breath exhaled from the back of her throat, an exasperated gasp, like part of her soul was seeping out. She looked at her mother, her expression blank.

'Eyes on the road.' Said Moira.

Heather did as she was told, Heather always did what she was told.

'I don't know what you were thinking? I don't know what you see in that boy anyway, nothing but a feckless wanker! You only ever think of yourself, that's your problem, you're inconsiderate. Your father would be ashamed of you, whoring yourself out like a slut. & to such a mouth-breathing cretin? Well, that's the last we'll be seeing of that pig-fucker!'

Heather was gripping the steering wheel so hard that her knuckles were turning white.

'What's wrong with you girl?'

'Aaaaaaaaaaaaaaaaaaaaaaaarrrrrrrrrrrrrgggggggg-gghhhhhhhhhhhhhh.'

Heather was screaming at the top of her lungs. Stamping the accelerator to the floor. She pulled a sharp left on the wheel, driving them straight into a tree.

They both survived the crash. Heather with a fractured arm, & superficial bruising to legs & face. Moira had been put in a full body cast. & when Heather first went to see her, there was a string of expletives far beyond anything which Heather had ever heard from her mother before. The Dr reassured her that these things can happen with traumatic brain injury, but that she was recovering well, & would be home soon. Heather had responded by putting a chair through the window of a vending machine. Slumped on the floor in amongst the broken shards. The nurses had to prise the chocolate bars out of her hands. They had lost the house but John had bought a little, two-floor, semi-detached, bungalow for them. As they pushed Moira out of the hospital, in her wheelchair & neck brace, she had refused to so much as look at them.

‘I’m going to rip your cock off, you fat useless cunt!’

Moira was perpetually sitting in the living room, through which John had to walk to get from the hall to the kitchen. In the hall there were stairs up to the second floor where John spent most of his time. He loathed walking through the living room, had picked up a mini fridge for his bedroom, even though, having lost his job, he couldn’t afford it. After having had just spoon-fed Moira, Heather was in the kitchen doing the dishes. He kissed her neck, walked over & opened a cupboard. Neither of them choosing to mention what her mother had just said, because it happened every time John walked through the living room.

‘Hey babe, there was a half pack of chocolate digestives in here this morning?’ John didn’t ask where they had gone, he didn’t need to.

‘Look I’m sorry alright, it’s just...’

‘It’s OK, look I’m not angry. I don’t want to make you feel guilty, honestly, I just don’t think you understand how bad our financial situation is. We simply can’t afford to keep buying this much food. I’m trying to cut back too.’

‘I get it, honestly. I’m sorry.’ Heather wrapped her arms around his waist & snuggled her head into his shoulder. ‘I love you so much!’ She said squeezing him tighter, looking up at him with doe eyes. John paused for a moment, then said,

‘I love you too!’

Then she let him go & went back to doing the dishes, & John went to fix himself a snack.

‘Is there any reason why the toaster is in the fridge?’ He asked, holding the fridge door open.

‘Oh right, so that’s where it went. I’m sorry, it’s these pills. That’s ridiculous! I don’t know what I’m doing half the time.’ Said Heather.

John put the toaster back on the counter, shaking his head. Loaded up a plate & walked back through the living room on the way up the stairs.

'I know what you're doing up there, all day! Yanking yer fuckin' plums!'

'The reason I'm going upstairs Moira, is so that I don't strangle you!'

'The only thing you're choking is your chicken!'

'Leave her alone.' Chimed in Heather, coming through from the kitchen. 'She can't help it!'

'Don't talk nonsense, of course she can!'

'You're a pair of fat, useless, cunts! I'm gonnae stab yer fuckin' eyeballs out while yer asleep!'

'Och shut it, you can't even get oot yer chair, ya numpty,' said John.

'Don't set her off,' said Heather

'Set her off? She's always like this.'

'You're a fucking dead man!' Said Moira, a slight spray of spittle forcefully ejected from behind tight lips. Her vicious, beady little eyes, fixed on him. Even though immobilised, she was a fearful sight. A witch-like skeletal face, emanating palpable hatred, with high arched eyebrows, prominent cheek bones, & rat-like yellow smokers' teeth. Unable to break her gaze, John slowly edged his way out of the room. After that John fell into the habit of drinking cheap cider, while playing massive multi-player online games, rarely leaving the second floor, wearing loud headphones every time he had to walk through the living room. Not even looking in Moira's direction.

A couple of days later, at Heather's insistence, John was trying to share his laptop with Moira. As John was putting it on her lap, her face was close up to his armpit. Heather watched her mother shifting in her seat, with a wrinkled nose, wincing at his smell.

'What in the fuck am I supposed to do with this?' Said Moira.

'Well, there's all sorts of things that you can do. You can watch movies, listen to music, look for things you're interested in. But I thought you might like to play solitaire. Look, here you go!'

'You like solitaire mum! Until you get the strength back in your arms, this will be a lot easier.'

Moira said nothing. Heather smiled at John to say that he'd done well, & was excused. Heather sat with her for a while, explaining how to turn it on, enter the passwords, how to browse, & play games. John went through to the kitchen, & Heather followed him in.

'We just have to take it one step at a time, she'll come around.' Said Heather. The expression on John's face said, 'you can't possibly believe that?' But he said nothing, when from the living room came...

'WHAT THE FUCK IS THIS?!!'

The pair of them rushed through to see what had happened. Moira looking utterly appalled. On the screen was an advert for an adult dating sight, with a woman stretching open her vagina.

'Oh, it's just a pop up,' said John.

'Get it the fuck away from me!' Said Moira slapping the laptop to the ground. John, protectively picked it up, checking it was intact.

'You're a dirty evil fucking cunt! Get the fuck away from me!'

Wordlessly John took the laptop, & went back upstairs, Heather followed. Moira sat staring after them, at the open door. After several minutes, Moira could hear their loud voices echoing down from above. She could hear the floorboards creaking, as they paced back & forth. She could hear intermittent statements from John, as he was getting more & more upset. 'You're fucking blind!' 'I can't take this!' 'I've had enough!' 'She has to go!' This went on for several minutes before Heather came down the stairs, John shouting after her...

'& it doesn't help with you eating me out of house & home as well.'

'You know I can't help it!' She said, in tears. Heather came up to Moira & bent down on her knees, putting her head in her lap. Her mother gently stroking her hair.

'It's alright darling, I won't let him hurt you! You're my precious girl, I won't let him do anything to you! I'll look after you, don't you worry! You can do so much better than him!'

The response didn't come as a surprise, it was the speed of the reply that was truly breath taking. Seemingly spring-loaded, & ready to fire off without a moment's hesitation. Heather had been waiting for an opportune moment, wanted to get her mother out of the house first, & speak to her alone. She was waiting for the first glimmer of positivity, & while pushing her mother along Sauchiehall street, Moira pointed out a pretty mural on the wall, & smiled, saying,

'Look at the kittens!'

'Mum, I'm pregnant.'

'When's the abortion?'

They walked on in silence, along the pedestrian zone, till they came to Hope street. Standing there waiting for the green man, Heather watched as the buses & lorries passed them by. & on some strange impulse her arms went to shove the handles of Moira's wheelchair, & she had to stop herself from pushing her mother out into heavy traffic. & by the time she got home John was already upset.

'Why are you wasting money on taxi's?' John asked Heather.

'If you think I'm getting in a car with her driving, you're more of a fucking idiot than I ever gave you credit for!' Said Moira.

'Why are you going into town?'

'We never get to leave the house; we're stuck in here like prisoners.' Said Heather.

'& I had to go to Marks & Spencer's to get my bits.' Said Moira, in her condescending, vowel quivering, tone.

'Get your bits?' Said John rifling through their shopping. 'Salmon?' Are you crazy, you have no idea how much we can't afford this!'

'You're a little skinflint, penny pinching cunt, aren't you?' Said Moira.

'Please mum, you're not helping. It was a once off!' Said Heather.

By which point John was already walking away, receding back into his online fantasy world of swords & sorcery. & as he walked up the stairs, he heard Moira behind him,

'Aye fuckin' typical, he's away to rip the heid aff it!'

After putting away the shopping, Heather fell asleep on the couch. A couple of hours later John felt Heather grip him by the shoulder, & by the time he got off his headphones she was already shouting at him.

'What the fuck do you think you're doing?'

'What?'

'I should report you to the social!'

'What are you talking about?'

John got up & followed her down the stairs, & into the sitting room, which was empty.

'Where's Moira?' He asked.

'Don't pretend like you don't fucking know!'

Heather pulled back the door to the walk-in cupboard in the living room, to reveal Moira inside, fast asleep in her chair.

'Jesus! Get her out of there!' Said John.

& as Heather pulled Moira gently out of the cupboard, Moira woke with a start.

'What are you two playing at? Trying to stuff me in the cupboard, were you? You fucking arseholes!'

Heather & John went back upstairs to the bedroom to talk, with Moira screaming insults at them from down below.

'Maybe she pushed herself in there?' Said John.

'That's nonsense, she can hardly lift her arm to wipe her face!'

'Well, maybe you pushed her in there?'

Heather hadn't thought about that, maybe she had pushed Moira in there? Better that, than under the wheels of an HGV. It gave her a flashback to that moment on Hope Street, & John read the change of expression on her face. Then when he pressed her on it, she went back downstairs, not wanting to admit, even to herself, what she had almost done.

John shut the front door with a bang, took off his jacket & put it on the coatrack at the bottom of the stairs. Meanwhile Heather was in the kitchen, having heard the front door, frantically rubbing the biscuit crumbs off her mouth, & clothes. John had become increasingly withdrawn over a period of time but today he was in a buoyant mood.

'Stupid fucking sack of shit!'

'Hi Moira.'

'Get fucked!'

When John appeared in the kitchen, Heather was emptying the garbage.

'Hey, look what I got!' John held up a bobble headed Deadpool doll. Heather was not impressed.

'How much did you waste on that then?'

'Shaun gave it to me.'

'I thought you were supposed to be out job hunting.'

'I was, I just dropped in on the way back. He's pretty cool, huh?

'Whatever.' Said Heather going back to the housework she was doing.

John sighed; his mood deflated he turned to walk away. When Heather had a sudden change of heart, & came & hugged him again.

'I'm sorry,' she said. 'I didn't mean to bitch at you. It's just cabin fever, you know? He is kind of cute. I love you!' Looking up at him with the same doe eyes.

This time John didn't say 'I love you' back. Instead saying, 'I thought I would stick him on the table by the front door, what do you think?'

Heather was slightly upset at him, but he didn't seem to notice.

'Sure.' She said, letting go of him.

But after she had finished in the kitchen she decided to go upstairs & talk with him. As she got to the bottom of the stairs she stopped. She noticed a strange smell; it was coming from the coatrack. On closer inspection she realised there was a woman's perfume coming from John's coat.

Heather's morning sickness finished after 14 week, & she started to show a couple of weeks after that. She had been having problems with her joints, & the hormones had been giving her mood swings. The arguments over food had stopped. Heather wondered whether it was because she was pregnant, or because there was so little food in the house anyway. & there were days that John couldn't play his computer because they didn't have enough money to put in the electricity meter. They rarely had money for the luxury of showers, & John's personal hygiene was never particularly great to begin with. They couldn't afford proper heating, & it had been getting extremely cold. They were all forced to wear extra layers. John had been spending less time at home, & when he was at home, he was becoming increasingly distant, an automaton, just following out his daily routine, even the tone of his voice had been getting increasingly flat. Heather spent most evenings reading to her mother by the light of cheap candles. It felt like they were living in a squat. One night, John was upstairs as usual, when he heard a commotion from the living room. He came quickly down the stairs, & opened the door, just in time to see Heather sweep an arm over the mantelpiece, scattering pictures & smashing ornaments to the floor, then overturning the coffee table, spilling drinks, & magazines.

'You're an evil, manipulative, poisonous cunt!' She screamed at her mother, before charging past John out into the hall & locking herself in the downstairs bathroom, next to the stairs. John followed her out, could hear violent sobs, as she struggled for breath, & knocked on the bathroom door.

'Honey, are you OK?'

'Fuck off!' Came the response.

John poked his head back around the door to check on Moira. & she was sitting in her chair, her shoulders shaking, her head bowed, crying in total misery. John had never seen her like this. Didn't even know she was capable of showing this kind of emotion. On impulse he went to her, & wrapped his arms around her, in an attempt to console her. When he suddenly felt a horrendous pain in his ear, she was biting him! With her rat-like yellow teeth. By the time he was able to pull his ear free, it was dripping with blood.

'What the fuck is wrong with you? You crazy old bitch!' Said John, clutching at his ear.

'This is all your fault! You turned her against me! You did this! You did this! You did this!'

A couple of days later John came home to a slap in the face. Heather had been waiting for him.

'I know what you've been up to! I brought your laptop downstairs so mum could play cards, & I know what you've been up to, you've been out with those fucking sluts! I know you've been cheating on me!'

Moira said nothing, but the expression she wore was defiantly gloating.

'What are you looking at her for, you can't blame her this time! Your laptop's been sitting upstairs in the bedroom!'

Without talking, John knelt down at the laptop & opened up a video file, from the camera inside the Deadpool doll out in the hall.

'Look, he's been spying on us! Turn that off, turn that off!' Said Moira, getting agitated.

On the video, through the open door you could see Heather asleep on the couch, & out came Moira, limping into the hall, but walking on her own two feet, a packet of chocolate biscuits in one hand, going into the downstairs toilet. When she re-emerged, she'd flushed about a third of the packet. The next clip showed her spraying perfume on John's coat. & the third showed her painfully limping up the stairs to the bedroom, so that she could go on John's laptop, & pretend to be him, & send emails to girls on dating websites, in an attempt to tear them both apart. Once the videos were finished Heather turned to look at Moira, who like a little child, turned her head away refusing to acknowledge what she had done.

Within a month, they'd found a place for Moira in an old-folks home. John got himself a new job, & their standard of living rose considerably. Without Moira in their lives, Heather stopped eating compulsively all the time, & John came out from behind his computer screen. & they started to live exactly the kind of life that Heather had always dreamed they could, going away on holidays together to tropical locations, relaxing, & having fun. They had a healthy baby girl, & Heather made the most solemn promise to herself that she would never treat her daughter the way that her mother had treated her. & every once in a while, she would go to visit Moira, who was the terror of her old-folks home. Telling everybody what to do, she even had a young volunteer who was happy to be ordered about, brushing her hair, helping her put on her pearls, standing in attendance like Heather used to do. & though she complained about how her ungrateful daughter had shut her away 'in this hellhole.' It was quite clear to see that she was happier in this place, than she had been in a long time. & whenever she went to visit, John waited in the car. One day, after they'd been to visit Moira, as John was driving them home, he asked Heather to open the glove box. Inside was an engagement ring, a perfect copy of the one which Moira had so casually tossed out the window, even the black satin box was identical. Tears rolled freely down Heather's cheeks, because she couldn't remember ever having been so happy.

DESPERATION

I don't drink anywhere near as much as I once did, but it's still an issue. It killed my grandfather. Twice I found him vomiting blood, & had to call an ambulance, the second time he never came back from the hospital. My last drink was on the 17th of Jan, & tonight it's the 5th of March 2020, & I just took my first swig of rum. Rob Zombie's 'More Human than Human' is playing in the background, we're fucking going for it! My novel series was birthed on nights like this, frenetic creativity till the break of dawn! What? You think I'm going to grab people's attention with self-help books? You have to sugar the pill, with sex, & ultra-violence! Tension building, character development, metaphorical depth, I can't afford to fuck about.

Last Nov I was put under general anaesthetic, & they ripped out my back molar & wisdom tooth. A couple of days later I had to make an emergency appointment at my local dentist, where they explained that a spike from my jawbone was sticking into the base of my tongue, which meant I couldn't swallow. Not just swallow food, or liquid, unable to swallow at all. I devised a system with a ball of wax, to depress one side of my tongue, so that I could suck through a straw. But if I wanted to eat a bowl of rice, that took about forty minutes, & resulted in mushy wax balls filled with foodstuff, & a general spray of half masticated chunks, in every direction. Leaving me breathless, with heavy sweating, it was literally exhausting. But it taught me a fundamental truth about myself. When the shit hits the fan, I'm going to drink! Then I'll get my shit together, & put it aside, but when tragedy strikes (& fingers crossed that it doesn't) I'll hit the bottle. So, what has happened?

When you work in the field of personal development, you are ideally looking to work yourself out of a job. I won't go into detail on my work, but for the last seven years I've supported someone whose entire life was a cycle of hospital admissions for complex mental health issues. & his life has been transformed, he's independent on a level that nobody ever expected. & it's come to the point where I am going to have to walk away from the service. It's time for me to go out & find a new job, & my head is running over a thousand different possibilities. I am not catastrophising, or trying not to anyway. I am heeding my own advice to the best of my abilities, but being on the autistic spectrum, big life changes raise a lot of stress. My intention is to make this a once off & then snap straight back into the ketogenic lifestyle, I've done this before. Not the wisest of moves, just my way of blowing off steam, but I feel guilty as fuck. It takes a lot of willpower for me to keep my shit together. As soon as a significant problem presents itself, my first thought is invariably about committing suicide. & quite often I'll look at other people who have it worse off than me & think, yeah, I would already have killed myself if I had to go through what you are dealing with. I have been through some heavy fucking shit myself, beyond the self-imposed stuff, the existential crisis, etc. But I don't feel at liberty to talk about it because it involves other people, even writing under a pseudonym I'm not going to just sit here writing about some of the evil cunts I've had to endure. It's mostly just depressing as fuck anyway.

But, I'm in a situation right now. I released 'The Optimal Path' a few months back, & despite the fact that accredited counsellors have told me that it's 'excellent in many ways,' not one single member of the public is even aware of its existence. & my plan was, hopefully, with everything that I had released, to make enough to substitute for unemployment allowance, while I spent every waking hour writing these novels, which could be turned into Netflix movies, or something. & those would be the calling card, for the Optimal Path, the Poetry of Chaos, etc. This might sound like straight up manipulation, but I'm telling you the honest fucking truth, the thoughts running through my mind as I'm listening to the Dark Knight on the bus home from work, are of the 'Aurora Shooter.' I believe my novels, my writing could have redirected those events, could have gotten through to him before he did what he did, because I know what it's like to feel like that. & maybe there is fuck all that I could have done to stop that, but maybe these books can stop the next kid from picking up a gun. Can make them see, just for an instant that I am thinking of them, I am looking right at them, right at you! You are not alone, that's all you need to know, to truly see, in your soul, you are not alone. Just that, one piece in a jigsaw puzzle, can change lives, change worlds. Recognition, understanding, real, true, heartfelt compassion. & I have just a little over one week to make these dreams come true, because I'm going to have to get a new job, my time, my focus is going to be swamped. I'm trying to buy time; I'm screaming out to the world for help, I need people to share these books. All I need are just a few bucks to keep the lights on. I want to throw all my time into writing these novels. I will keep going regardless, but if I can buy time then those might be the precious moments which avert a real tragedy. That's the fire that I've lit under my ass, that's why I'm drinking. That's why there's no escaping it tonight, I just have to throw my cards on the table. & in vino veritas, as they say. Rage Against the Machine's, 'Killing in the Name' is playing in the background. My neighbour was banging on the wall, doing DIY, they started it!

Events in America are strangely distorted when seen through the lens of someone in Scotland. When I was a kid, I used to think that the soft focus which they used in 'Cheers' was what life was like in America. I was looking forward to one day, visiting the 'soft focus world' in my imagination. & I was so disappointed when I found out that it didn't exist. I can imagine an autistic kid being disappointed to find out they didn't all have three fingers, & yellow skin like the Simpsons. America likes to think of itself as the greatest country on earth, but somewhere in the British psyche America only exists to provide them with entertainment. From the Wild West to the gang shootings. We get to live our affluent, mundane, drizzle filled lives without the threat of drive-bys, bears, or rattle-snakes. But this effect for me is best exemplified by serial killers. Because Dahmer, Bundy, Gacy have this glitzy, almost Rockstar vibe. Kids in the U.K can barely imagine having the kind of hardware they brought to the Columbine shootings. A kid with green hair shooting up a cinema? There's something too over the top about it all, but the Dunblane massacre, Fred West, the Yorkshire Ripper, they all make me physically disgusted. No glitz, no glamour, it's just fucking horrible! It genuinely makes my skin crawl. Because it's a lot closer to being real, when it's happening around you. So, what is that effect like when you take it to a greater extreme, people in Africa for example? Well, there's always a famine somewhere isn't there? Refugees somewhere? How quickly does it become 'not my fucking problem?' Take for example these beautifully constructed heart tugging adverts about children dying in war torn countries. I went to see 'Parasite' twice, 'The Lighthouse' in-between, ('The Witch,' also by Robert Eggers, is one of the greatest horrors I've ever seen.) The same advert plays every time, & the first time I can barely look at the screen, third time, I'm barely bothering to look up from my paper. But I watch myself, my reactions to these things, & I watch other people, it's not just me, it's human nature, to try to give as little of a fuck as possible, it's what stops you from giving away everything you have. It always comes down to the same problem of barriers, how open you are, how closed you are, how giving, or not. The Coronavirus has brought up a lot of racial assaults, as Ki-Woo might say, it's 'so metaphorical' (besides being appalling, obviously.) But I'm on the verge of giving away everything so that I can give everything of myself, I'm walking that line. & I am putting myself in the place of the families who lost loved ones because of an avoidable American mass-shooting, without putting it in soft focus, I'm looking at it as objectionably as the Dunblane Massacre, it's not just something that happens on TV. It happens to real people, & extreme events ruin lives, on a level that we turn a blind eye to. But working on a suicide hotline you are overwhelmed with the aftermath of rapes, abortion, murder, family bereavement, mental health crisis, etc, etc, etc. & to think that any of it is preventable, that there's anything that you could do to stop it, to change people's lives, so that they were never touched by tragedy in the first place? That's the pressure that I have put on my shoulders, & that's why I'm drinking tonight, or at least, that's my excuse. What's yours?

Korn, 'Blind' is playing, that means we really are not fucking about! 'Good God' is my favourite song of theirs, but I never got to see it live, during the 'Life is Peachy' tour I missed them because of head trauma, it wasn't my first concussion either. I came off a skateboard, my mum finding me in a pool of blood in the street. I woke looking at an orange bag, 'I know it belongs to somebody, it means something, but what?' My friend from Inverness had been staying for a week, I'd forgotten all about it. Had absolutely no memory of ever being in a hospital? How did I end up like this? Is it autism? Or is it, chronic traumatic encephalopathy? I try not to play the blame game; I just have to get on with it. The truth is I'm already fucked, the idealistic image I had of making money from writing was a soft-focus fantasy. The truth is I probably couldn't change anything, it's all just wishful thinking. But I have believed in it, more deeply than anything else I've ever tried to do in my life, & I've felt the benefit for it. It's almost irrelevant what the objective is, being focused gets you closer to a fuller version of yourself. That's right, I beat you to it, this is all irrelevant, a self-indulgent fantasy. I can go fuck myself. But I can tell you what I hoped, wished, wanted. Just to help. Help reduce the needless suffering in the world, that was all. To help people from hurting themselves, & murdering each other, that was all I was trying to do.

OK well, the writing till dawn thing never happened, it's

the following day, & I'm half way between the walking dead, & a badger's arse, which is to say, pretty rough. Last year when I was about to go under general anaesthetic I was wondering, what if I die? & it does happen, people under general anaesthetic do die on occasion. & it might sound like catastrophising, but for the suicidal part of my brain, it was more like wishful thinking. But there was only one problem, I hadn't released 'The Optimal Path.' That was the one thing I needed to do before I died, & to this day, not one member of the general public has bothered to read it. But on some level that doesn't matter, I can now go to my grave knowing that I got it out there, my response, to this thing they call life. A message of hope, & universal love, despite the drizzle, the ostracism, & the blades under my throat. I'm not giving up; it just isn't an option. You just have to pick yourself up, & go again! I'm going to keep writing till I get noticed, I'm going to enrol for marketing seminars, I'm going to use social media, I'm going to suck off the devil while maintaining eye contact, if that's what it takes. & when it comes to peace of mind, there's nothing more I need to do, but this isn't about me anymore. It's bigger than that. I've made it bigger than that, in my soft-focus fantasy, I'm trying to save lives. & if I am burdened with alcoholism, I might as well harbour the aspirations of one day becoming a semi-acknowledged writer. & I'm still in my little bubble right now, just talking into the wind, & maybe one day I'll miss it? Maybe being acknowledged would be the worst thing that ever happened to me? My bubble popped, becoming a pastiche of myself, opening the door to an avalanche of hatred & criticism? Because nothing corrupts like success, let me be a failure, just a little bit longer, I'm not ready to get out of bed quite yet, still clinging to the comfort of my anonymity.

As you can see, I never did quite kick those grandiose narcissistic fantasies. One day I'll be catapulted to meteoric success, I'll be surrounded by cocaine & sluts. One day everybody will see me for who I really am, they'll acknowledge my magnificence. It's a twofold problem, a psyche struggling to come to terms with its relationship with omnipotence, & a society geared up to manipulate that part of you. Start a garage band, get on MTV, become a multi-millionaire, all your problems solved, all the pussy you can eat. Wait, hold on, stuck in a call centre, chasing after the illusion of social mobility, fuck it, I'll just kill a bunch of people, then the world can't help but notice me. Because you are part of universal consciousness, you really are like a god, you could change the lives of people around you, for better or worse. I believe that making people truly empowered removes their need to make desperate expressions, to seek acknowledgement in the most detrimental of ways, mass slaughter, & suicide by cop. It's like a martial artist, who no longer feels intimidated, not having to make a display of how tough they are. It's feeling invisible, feeling powerless, overwhelmed, which makes people desperate, which causes them to lash out. The wrong thing to do is to vilify people for feeling like that, branding them as evil, their behaviour as unthinkable. Because as deranged as it might seem, there is a twisted logic behind the mass shooter, that's why it keeps on happening. You can't stand on the outside pointing fingers, like trying to solve any social-problem, the first thing you need is empathy! Why do people feel the need to act out these violent fantasies? It's a multi-layered problem, but at the heart of it there's an expression of suffering, a disconnection. So, that's where I am starting, instead of running from the gunfire, I'm running toward it, trying to get to people before they pull the trigger. Not sitting in judgement, but offering compassion, understanding, looking you right in your fucking eye! I get it, I genuinely do! Homicidal insomnia, night after night, trying to push the ideas out of your head, guns, blades. There weren't semi-automatic rifles in my house, but there were shotguns. Picturing heads exploding like watermelons, hearing the screams of my classmates, the feel of a kitchen knife sinking into someone's torso, blood dripping on the floor, as the smoke clears. Half-awake up the back of the class, daydreaming again. If I had access to machine-guns when I was in my teenage years, we would not be having this conversation right now. I'd be dead, & so would a lot of other people. I'm not saying this to scare you, I'm saying this to people who know what it's like, to feel overwhelmed with violent fantasies. You are not a monster! You are not alone, in an uncaring world! Existence is not fucked, & you do not need to resort to violence as an expression of suffering! There is a light at the end of the tunnel, a world beyond your existential crisis, there is love, & joy, & beauty. There is more to life than you are currently aware, there is another way to see the world. I had to go through the fall, to get to this place, but it exists, it is possible, change is possible.

& when you are closed off to the world, when you are numb, the scariest thing is opening up, to genuinely care. But you are generating your own fantasy, you are stuck in a world of your own creation, & it's time to snap out of it. It's time for the entire of mankind to snap the fuck out of it. We're not all going to be rock stars, but why would you want to be? They end up being shut away from the world, overdosing in their attempt to self-medicate, dying on the toilet, or blowing their own head off. It's excess, it's extremes, it's an imbalance, it's fucking stupid, & you know it! Society is constructed around false ambition, & the lie of social mobility. I know what it's like to be the life of the party, for the room to light up when I walk in, & my ego fed on it, being the centre of attention, but ultimately, I found that was hollow too. People only build you up, to tear you down. It's a pointless game, a rollercoaster, & like a drug high, it can't last. We're all chasing after the wrong things, running on impulse, easily manipulated. There's no surprise that people are dissatisfied, & in that sense mass-shooters are just one symptom of a much bigger problem. Religion used to be at the core of people's lives, but that's been corrupted by paedophile priests, & TV evangelists, pocketing vast sums of money. Nobody trusts in authority anymore, & understandably so. But it's a case of throwing out the baby with the bathwater. We've lost our sense of community, reverence, humility, purpose. We live unfocused lives, & I'm not trying to build a religion, or telling you to go to church, but there's great wisdom to be found in ancient texts, life changing merit in meditative practices, & if there was one single word which I could drill into your forehead, then it would be 'BALANCE!!!' It's too simple, too easily overlooked, but it's the answer to everything, navigating your way through life, the interplay of extremes, peace. Our attention is always somewhere over the hill, not on where we are, what is happening, because it requires focus, on a level that our society doesn't teach. Because consumerism has decided that it needs to instil a thirsting ambition in us, it wants you to be endlessly aspiring, as you sit in your factories, dreaming about what life might be like, if only? If only I was famous, if only I was rich, if only I was the one getting all the freaky sex! Psychological mass-marketing preys on your animalistic impulses, your fears, like social media, it's always promising, never delivering. Mankind is chasing the dragon, & they are fucking up the planet in the process. Everybody knows it, but it's another case of 'not my fucking problem.' & I'm as lazy & apathetic as everybody else, I'm no shining light, I'm a fucking reject, probably just the same as you! Overlooked, & ignored, irrelevant. But I have found reverence, connection, focus, love, through open awareness, I have found the true importance of balance. I have freed myself of existential depression, psychotic rage, & any number of mental health issues, by simply letting go, & finding purpose in the service of others, it's at the core of everything I write, the desire to help, to instil belief in those who are lost. Because I recognise that particular hell, I've crawled my way out of it, to show you that it can be done, & to explain to you that a show of violence is a display of weakness, it's fragility, not strength. You need to find a positive outlet for your suffering, you need to talk about your problems, you need to find a purpose that's worthy of devotion, whether that's creative, or simply productive in a way that makes the world a better place, you need something which allows you to grow, & transcend the version of you that feels stuck, & frustrated.

On a personal level, I'm not looking for acknowledgement, I'm not chasing after wealth. I would rather stay in the shadows, writing under a pseudonym, & I love watching the way I've progressed over the years, but I'm not doing it for people's opinions of me. I'm trying to make a success of these books despite myself. I'm trying to force these books into the public sphere, even though I want no part of it. I don't want to hear a single word from the public at large, I don't want any involvement with fame whatsoever, it's the last thing on earth I want. I don't want expectations; I don't want pressure. I don't want contracts; I don't want to have anything to do with financial matters. I just want to be left alone, but given the nature of what these books are intended to do, that simply isn't an option. So here I am, on my knees, in old school supplication, begging for your help. I need word of mouth, to get these books into the right hands. & they may never stop a mass shooting, but they are aimed at the same problems of which mass-shootings are a direct symptom. Problems which are happening in psyche's all around you. 'The Optimal Path' is the answer to the existential crisis that nearly killed me. It is a blueprint for how to function in life, produced from trial & error, a whole lot of error. & constructed with wisdom from ancient texts, sociologists, gurus, psychiatrists, advice for problems which every single person on the planet has to face at some point, all condensed & simplified. I'm virtually giving you the cheat codes for life, & I'm throwing it away for under a fiver, because I just want enough money to write full time, & to get the message out there. & the more I write, the more clearly I see it, what it is I'm trying to do, what the underlying patterns of the world really look like. & the deeper my sense of compassion becomes, for others, & for my own failures. Because failure is part of the process, it's how we learn. But if your failure ends in suicide or mass murder, then somewhere along the line things kind of got a little out of hand, didn't they? But it's not just one individual that is at fault, it's the whole system that makes people fucked up. It's because of the rat race, the corporations, the faceless automaton which mass consumerism programs you to be, pumping you full of chemicals, hollow aspirations, the abject failure of organised religion, the gadgets which replaced your human interactions, it's all of that shit. & throw in teen hormones, existential angst, & some military grade weaponry, & you've got yourself a serious fucking problem! & I really don't want to ask for your help, but I'm fast approaching the point of desperation!

HONESTY

I can't help but reflect on the nature of this endeavour, & believe me, I recognise the naivety of someone trying to fix the world's problems. Over the last few days, I've watched a stream of videos online about the housing crisis in Hong Kong, & skid row in downtown LA. People just lying in the streets, surrounded by trash, shitting in buckets, even the U.N has had to step in, because it's worse than 3rd world conditions. Back to back with videos showing the inside of these gaudy 55 million-dollar mansions, with their own helicopter pads, night clubs, hair salons, & polo fields. It's hard to countenance that kind of disparity, or how the ultra-rich can surround themselves with such opulence, when people all over the world are literally starving to death. They say the major reason people become homeless is from a catastrophic loss of family. When you look at all this, it's hard to imagine there is much of anything you could do about it. Maybe the person who owned that mansion is a philanthropist who achieved more to help people than I can ever dream? & this ran over into videos about notorious prisons, & I ended up watching the sentencing of a kid that stole a six-year-old out of her bed, took her into a forest, raped, & murdered her. In the background you could hear the shrieks of her family, it was deeply disturbing, especially in light of the account of how utterly callous the perpetrator was, laughing, indifferent. I could write for a thousand years & never create anything to alter a psyche such as that. To be honest I can barely even imagine that such a person exists. & I've talked about this elsewhere as well, but I see a clear distinction between the actions of a sexual sadist, the serial killer type, & an active shooter. For me, the spree killer is at the opposite end of the spectrum, instead of hiding in the shadows, it's an open act of defiance, against existence itself. It's the result of years of pent up frustration, a feeling of powerlessness, turned to hate, finally erupting into an extreme act of violence. I'm trying to create something of an early intervention, but going down this path may actually be about something else, something even bigger. The spree killer is actually just the tip of the iceberg, & perhaps by trying to address it, what I'm actually doing is trying to illustrate some of the fundamental flaws within contemporary society.

& ultimately, I have to ask the question, of who the fuck am I, to criticise? I'm a nobody, soon to be out of work, virtually penniless, somebody who invariably turns to drink when the going gets tough. I'm a flawed individual, & I don't even want to pretend for a second that I am not. But I've looked over the edge of the abyss. I've had my life shattered, been forced to become aware of my own narcissistic delusions. I've experienced loss, that I'm not even in the least bit prepared to talk about here. I've survived, & rebuilt my whole existence. Overcome an existential crisis, twelve years of suicidal ideation, a prolonged psychotic episode, come to terms with my autism, my neuroticism, etc. & along the way I've created a battle hardened, pragmatic philosophy, scrapped together from a thousand different sources, which has done far more than just help me endure, it's brought a rich & sustained joy into my life that very few people in the history of mankind have ever experienced. A sense of peace that has become a fundamental part of who I am as a human being. & I do lose focus from time to time, go off the rails slightly, my life is far from perfect. But over time I've noticed myself becoming more resilient, & sure of myself, & my intentions. I want to help transform people's lives, & I know I can, I'm absolutely certain of it! More than just because of what I've been through, & the things I've learned along the way, it's because I care, & that's what people need, they need someone who genuinely cares.

As much as I might feel like I need to present myself as an exceptional individual, who has overcome extraordinary obstacles, just to make people listen to me. The truth is, that is nowhere near as important as simply being open & honest. I am scared about what the future holds, not just for me, but for everyone on this planet. The Holocene era is over ladies & gentlemen, 12,000 years of climatic stability is at an end, that's where the drizzle went. We've taken it for granted, & 'our economies & political systems are unconsciously predicated on the belief that nature will remain a benign & regular provider of the conditions we need to thrive,' (David Attenborough) fresh water, bountiful seas, regular seasons, the quality of soil. If you go back 1500 years the climatic fluctuations were truly catastrophic, this period of stability is the anomaly. Startling changes are happening all over the world, the rainforests are burning, & Milan is currently on lockdown because of the Coronavirus. You already know my perspective on social media, & the psychological impact it's going to have on the next generation. Then there's the inevitability of the birth of artificial intelligence on the horizon, that's something to look forward to. Have you ever seen a 3d rendering of earth tailing behind the sun? The sun is basically a projectile, hurtling through the cosmos at thousands of miles per hour, a cosmos filled with black holes, & vast meteorites. & there's always the potential for a super-volcano, like Yellowstone, to completely fuck us up out of nowhere. Not to mention the ever-present threat of nuclear war. The reality is that I'm not going to stop the world's problems, but I can maybe help you stop needlessly tearing your hair out, over insignificant shit. I can maybe help you stop hurting yourself unnecessarily. I can maybe amuse you with my idiocy, or signpost you to life changing books, & cherry-picked advice from gurus, & psychologists.

& maybe the zombie apocalypse won't happen in our lifetime, but death is coming, for all of us, there's no avoiding that most fundamental truth. & I don't want people to waste their lives, trapped in rumination, focused on petty grievances, fighting against themselves. & there is an ulterior motive to all this (no it's not freaky sex,) it's that if I can concentrate on helping eradicate the unnecessary suffering in other people's lives, then I can learn self-mastery in the process. & the occasional drink aside, I can honestly say that process has been life changing. But the real challenge is to try & impart the huge moments of realisation that shaped my perspective over the years, some of which were through psychedelics as I'm sure you can hear in the way that I talk. I'm a modern-day hippy, with a street-goth slant. Peace & love may be the answer but it's a fairly limp-wristed message, people need something which is more pragmatic, with a sharper edge. These days if you want someone to listen to your philosophy, you have to stab it through their neural cortex! We're beyond the point where we can afford to fuck about! There's a lot of shit that we're going to have to rethink from the ground up, & don't come at me with your genocidal ideologies, whether it's left wing or right wing, the body count speaks for itself. & maybe I'm overreacting, maybe I just sound like a doomsayer, because I've watched too many Youtube videos, but there are changes I can see with my own eyes. The streets are filled with homeless. The wind has been howling for months, & every time you turn on the TV there's images of towns which have been flooded out. Brexit is upon us, Trump is in the Whitehouse, Bojo is in number 10, it's a fucking shitshow, let's be honest! & I don't want to stand on anybody's toes, maybe you are a Trump supporter, I honestly couldn't care less about all that tribal nonsense, but it's your turn to be honest, would you buy a used car off that guy?

I saw an article today about two women arrested for fighting over toilet paper in Sydney, they were panic-buying because of the Coronavirus. & perhaps there won't be a third world war, or a world ending meteor strike in my lifetime, but one thing is almost certain to happen over the coming years, the viral pandemics are going to get substantially worse! As it happens, there is an asteroid heading for earth as we speak, it'll reach us around April the 29th. A global killer needs to be bigger than 0.6 miles across, & this one is 2.5. They tend to just fly past, but you never know? I'm not really trying to freak you out; I'm trying to show you that I can empathise. Life is scary, even before you take all your own personal problems into the equation, you don't need to add catastrophising to your list of problems. & it's more than understandable why a person would choose to put up barriers, would rather spend their time plugged into entertainment technology, turning a blind eye to the people camping out in doorways. But the barriers which we build, tend to wall us in, emotionally, psychologically. When you fall into binary thinking, you create extremes. I am right, & you are wrong, the rich get richer, the poor get poorer. We need an open dialogue, to find moderation, & the problem is that people's perspectives are becoming calcified. They are drawn into echo-chambers where their ideologies are reinforced. & when taken to the extreme, little girls are getting blown apart at pop concerts. Everything can be brought back to the concept of balance, & the nature of the yin-yang symbol. Because everything follows the same patterns, of waves, & cycles, a rise & fall, the interplay of chaos & order.

It is precisely because I am so insignificant, that I am free. I am free to tell the truth. I might be wrong, I almost certainly am wrong about any number of things, but I am free to learn from my mistakes, free to grow & evolve. & I want to share this process with the world, over the years. I want to bring you into my world, & write all the time. I am not playing a role, I am not a politician, I am not a guru, I am free to fluctuate, & explore new modes of self-expression. I am free to play, & that's what I want to bring into your life, I want to entertain you, almost more than I want to share my philosophy, because I just want to have fun. But I want to keep it real, I want to help people too, help them be more at peace within themselves so that they feel free to have fun as well. Sure, there's all sorts of scary shit going on in the world, but it's also filled with wonders, humour, art, excitement, passion. Being alive is fucking amazing, when you really are alive, fully present,

& focused. That's why I was having a serious dig at social media, it's because it's stealing away so much of people's ability to connect with the real world. The same with narcissistic delusions, sacrificing your true self, that's no kind of existence. Neuroticism too, ruminating over insignificant things, spiralling loops of thought, that's just another trap. I want to set people free, I want to help you find peace, & joy, & the self-belief to go out & find a meaningful purpose. I want to help you envision alternatives, because these are the things I want in my own life. This is what I am training myself to do. & I struggle to balance my lifestyle when I'm put under serious stress, but that just makes me human. & every time I fuck up, I try to analyse it, pick out the problems, research whatever advice there is out there in the world, & then try to capture it for others, & for myself. It's because I'm a fuck up, that I'm the right person to be writing about this stuff. I'm not a dusty old professor, this is the perspective from the front line! & because we are free to talk about anything, then as long as the world keeps turning, then we'll never run out of things to talk about. This isn't just a plea for help, I'm opening up an invitation to you, to join me in the experience of this thing we call life. I want to write book, after book, after book, & they will vary wildly in content, filled with fuck only knows, stories, poetry, comedy, horror, romance, adventure. I want to capture your imagination, & enrich your life in countless ways.

The U.S.A just shut its borders to mainland Europe because of the Coronavirus, shit's getting real guys. Major sporting events like the Premier league, & the 6 nations have been completely suspended; I've never seen anything like this in my lifetime. The estimate is over 480,000 deaths in the next 6 to 7 months. Why toilet paper though? I googled it, it's completely irrational behaviour, just the onset of generalised panic which is causing people to stockpile things, & toilet paper is durable. & when the shelves are emptying everybody else is panicking because they don't want to have to go without. Aah, aah, gotta buy stuff, aah. Human beings are just fucking ridiculous sometimes.

& the media are absolutely relishing all of this, because fear sells. & who runs these media conglomerates? Rich old fat cats, who have a vested interest in avoiding Covid-19, because they are at a higher risk than most. But down at street level there is a building sense of pressure on all sides, it seems like everybody is going through some sort of trauma at the moment. Losing loved ones, deterioration of physical, & mental health. My folks just back from the funeral of a close friend. Even the structure of the buildings around us seems to be collapsing, absentee landlords, ceilings caving in from broken pipes, skipping through the puddles. Kids bullying each other, everything escalating, till adults start to get involved, death threats flying about. The stress is mounting, & things seems to be getting out of control. & absolutely everything is about the Coronavirus right now, it's on every channel. Every conversation seems to rotate around it.

I'm just back from the supermarket, half expecting to see a pair of old dears rolling about on the floor, fighting over a pack of Kleenex. But that motherfucker was SOLD OUT!!! It's like we're expecting a hurricane, a shitstorm on the horizon? I should maybe have brought out a paperback, on soft-ply tissue paper, covered in eastern philosophy, & self-help material. Personal growth, wit, & wisdom, the ultimate toilet book, silky & absorbent. It's hard to stay calm when we're constantly bombarded with threats to our own mortality, & the potential threat of losing our loved ones. Added to which the U.S.A has just closed its borders to the UK & Ireland as well. We struggle when life gets complex, what people need is simplicity, & you'd struggle to find a bigger simpleton than me! But in all seriousness, the search for simplicity has been something of a life's work for me. I need simplicity because I am sensitive, I get easily overwhelmed, & structure helps calm me down. Over time I've been able to find a certain frequency, a perspective that feels grounded. & I keep finding correlation between lived experience, & the deep wisdom of great philosophers. Part of that is perhaps maturity, but more than that I feel as though I've made a very significant discovery, something I was only able to find when I stopped looking. My mind was clouded with thoughts, lost in perpetual cognition, the wrong method of approach. In a single moment of pure non-attachment, I stopped. & making that decision was like giving up on life itself. & in the echoing silence I heard my intuition, it had been present all along, but in my pride, caught up in headlong momentum, I had been ignorant of it. In that moment, over sixteen years ago, everything changed! The twelve years of suicidal ideation were over, there was an instant physical change inside my cranium, like a balloon filled with stress deflating. If it's clarity & insight that you seek, you must first learn to embrace stillness.

& now, as I follow this path, I'm starting to see patterns which were once obscured to me. I'm coming to understand myself, & the world, through fearless articulation, by trying to speak my truth. & through this process, the way I feel internally is changing, the way I feel about myself, & the nature of existence. The intellect tends to fall in love with itself, but what I'm doing is unlearning. To be truly creative you have to accept that you do not know, & it's deeply humbling. But I am simultaneously developing an extraordinary level of self-belief because my attention is focused externally. I am training myself to care more deeply, & only now, as I'm learning how to openly communicate, am I starting to realise the importance of the things which I have discovered, & their potential impact beyond my inner world. What I want to share with you is less a piece of inherited wisdom, & more a feeling, a sensation which is very prominent in my psyche at this moment. It's a sense of clarity, a certainty, a state of equilibrium, which comes from persistent focus. Because that's how you deal with thc complexity of life, the tragedy, & the suffering, alignment through self-awareness. & there's a significant piece of misinformation which you have to first comprehend, joy is not the outcome that you seek, it is the shining light which guides you, an ever-present part of you, often obscured by fear, anxiety, & lack of focus. For example, it's humour that breaks through a state of desperation, a single moment of levity can be truly life altering. Such as a well-timed piece of dark humour, which only your best friend could deliver. & in that moment you might feel like telling them to fuck off, but there is a connection, a life-giving breath of air. & once again, you have to find the balance in everything I say, you shouldn't suppress emotions, & try to convince yourself that you are joyous when you are not. To overcome inner turmoil, & reclaim the disavowed parts of the self, you have to be brutally honest, for the sake of personal growth.

But that spark of joy, that love for life, that's your true-self. It's what we lose sight of amid the complexity of consumer culture. With these books I am expressing my authentic self, in the hope that it reflects with others, can help awaken something in you. & the truth is I went about it the wrong way, I took the long way around, I took the road of trial & error. I beat myself into submission, & I genuinely don't know how much of it was necessary. But there was nobody there to simplify things for me, so that's what I'm trying to do for you, for all of you. The world is overloaded with information, these days most people aren't prepared to sit & read challenging material. So, I'm going to pulp it up, & spoon feed you. But more importantly, I want us to have fun, I want to make you laugh, about the absurdity of life, & all its foibles. Because I want to spend my life in that state, of creative, playful, adventure. Writing stories, mixing genres, taking you on a rollercoaster of emotions. Constantly surprising myself with elaborate twists, & turns. To find joy, & deep fulfilment in your work, & a sense of purpose, by taking on the responsibility of trying to make the world a better place, that is the ideal for which I am striving. A life devoted to creative passion, helping to free others of their self-destructive patterns of behaviour, & focusing myself through that process.

& there are plenty of examples within humanist psychology, & great works of literature, of people with similar views to my own. The prominent psychologist Abraham Maslow described creativity & thinking of others as characteristics of the Self-Actualized person. Erich Fromm emphasised finding purpose, as a means to overcome man's sense of isolation. & that it is imperative to discover one's own sense of self, & one's own personal views, & value systems, rather than adhering to conventional or authoritarian norms. As far as I see it, that's what gives rise to the genocidal state, Nazi's, Communists, & terrorist alike. Don't follow anyone blindly, learn to think for yourself. High up on my reading list is Viktor Frankl's 'Man's Search for Meaning.' A prominent Viennese psychiatrist, held prisoner in Auschwitz who was able to observe how people coped with the experience. He came to believe that man's deepest desire is to search for meaning and purpose, as a way to transcend suffering and find significance in the art of living. & if you can't be arsed reading, these are actually recurring themes in the 'Toy Story' franchise. Children's stories are a rich source of archetypal characters. There are certain truths which we recognise on a deep fundamental level, & what I want to do is step through the page & slap people in the face. Because we're steeped in entertainment, & allegories, but people seem to have lost the connection, they don't see how it applies to them. It's just a book, it's just a movie, no! Being in your essence, the aim of the hero, is what Fromm describes as 'the person without a mask.' Your online avatar, your narcissistic false-self, your neuroticism, these are the masks which people wear, the prisons which we have built for ourselves.

A week later & Britain was on lockdown, my service suspended, me unemployed. & there are signs everywhere, not just people in face masks, literal signs. The ones on the motorway read 'STAY HOME SAVE LIVES,' in fluorescent yellow lights. & I'm listening to the 'Contagion' soundtrack as I write. Re-watched '28 Days Later' again the other day, I'm reading Stephen King's 'The Stand' obviously. I'm getting right into it! 'Will you please stand behind the line sir!' Social distancing, cues outside supermarkets. It's a Saturday night & I just sat on an empty bus through town, & it was totally dead, on a level that I've never seen, even on the rainiest Sunday. All the bars closed, shops closed, & where did all the homeless people go? Are they staying home, like everybody else? Was it all a ruse, were there really no homeless people at all? Or have the government gone & done something about it? & if so, why did it take a global pandemic for them to finally pull their finger out? Fear is rife! If only virologists knew that simply pulling a scarf over your face would work, they would have saved themselves a fortune in lab equipment! Old men are wearing sanitary pads on their faces, in the shops, which just about sums it up! & what comes next? Will there be riots, after the economic downturn? Will the terrorists, take inspiration from the way the West ground to a halt, closing its borders, creating a level of fear to which they could only aspire. Will their focus shift to viral weaponry? Are their men in caves, feeding bats to pigs as we speak?

& through all this I keep thinking to myself, 'you should not fuck with sparrows!' & I might be wrong, but the news presents the start of covid-19 as having come from the Wuhan Market in China. Because after having suffered an extreme famine, there were changes to the rules & regulations around which types of livestock were kept as food. Which meant animals which would not normally come into close contact with one another, are all forced into close proximity, creating a petri dish out of which we can expect pandemics to regularly appear. & how did that famine come about? Chairman Mao, back in the day decided that the Sparrows were eating all the grain, so they slaughtered them. Then without their natural predator to keep them in check, the locust swarms devastated their crops! & there's your life-lesson in all of this, fuck with the balance of nature at your extreme peril! We make simple assumptions. In our brains we create a caricature of reality, a strawman argument, without understanding the complexity of the situations which we are dealing with. Take left wing ideals for example, at their extreme we're talking about Stalinist (In truth, Lennonist) Russia. I watched a documentary recently called 'Night & Fog' about the Nazi concentration camps. I'll never get used to the sight of corpses getting pushed by a bulldozer. They had camps the size of cities, gas chambers, running night & day, mechanised slaughter at its most brutally efficient, & yet Stalin somehow managed to kill more people than Hitler? What kind of malice can you hide behind idealistic notions of brotherhood? A staggering amount, or so it would appear? & yet Mao's death toll is even bigger, & still rising! & the same lessons apply on an individual level, as on a societal one. When motivated by greed, anger, fear, & acting on oversimplified preconceptions, we can effectively cause a level of destruction in our lives, that we can't possibly conceive. & this applies just as much to our psyches, as it does our external environment. & I hope through adversity we can become stronger, more understanding, less xenophobic, misogynistic, wrapped up in our own petty bullshit. & instead find peace within ourselves, & cultivate a deeper level of respect for one another. But evidently, even the loftiest of ideals can be used as justification to commit genocide.

At the start of this book I said that part of the aim was to learn about 'overcoming fear, instead of choosing to be numb, allowing yourself to be vulnerable, being able to communicate, & then being able to connect with other people.' & to be completely without fear is not healthy. Children who murder animals, consistently tend to have a particular brain abnormality, a low level of arousal in the frontal cortex, an excess of theta waves, & thusly little to no fear of the consequences of their antisocial behaviour. But the life of a neurotic individual, can ultimately be controlled by fear. Again, it's about finding a healthy balance, learning how to set aside the counter-productive defence mechanisms, the self-medication, the self-harm, etc. & through writing this book I've certainly learned a lot more about narcissistic defence mechanisms. & it seems apparent to me that coming to understand yourself, is what allows you to communicate more freely with others. Our lives are constantly filled with distractions, & chatter, a constant stream of our own bullshit. & the only way to break out of that pattern is to find a moment of true stillness, to be fully present. There is a deep serenity within us that is always there, yet is perpetually overlooked. There is peace within you, but you have to train yourself to find it, to sustain it, & then share it, through your words, your actions, & your presence.

We are at the end of this book now, & I don't want it to stop. Is it strange that I feel that I'm having to say goodbye to an old friend? But this is really just the beginning, seek out the 'Optimal Path.' Whatever's going on with you, I hope things work out. Try not to beat yourself up, it is quite literally counter-productive. I wish you luck in all your endeavours, I hope you find meaning in life, a sense of purpose, & are able to more fully embrace your true-self. Look into cognitive distortions & start rationalising your perspective. Find clarity though stillness, be consistently self-aware, & learn to trust your intuition! Let joy be your guide, in the search for peace. I hope I've helped you come to understand more about yourself, as that is key to developing a deeper connection with others.

Take care,

Much love!

The Snow Hare

OTHER BOOKS

If you've enjoyed this, then please check out...

The Optimal Path

Book 2:

The Playmaker

Book 3:

The Walled Garden

or

The Poetry of Chaos

All available on Amazon, by T.S. Hare

& coming soon!!!

The Know it All

Travelling further down the optimal path, this book kicks to life with an explosive opening chapter entitled 'Gender.' Featuring more wicked little short stories. Packed with humour & ultra-violence. & on a personal level, capturing yet another profound evolution, in the literary career of The Snow Hare!

Printed in Great Britain
by Amazon